INSIGHT GUIDES

ALGARVE

POCKET GUIDE

◉ Walking Eye App

YOUR FREE EBOOK AVAILABLE THROUGH THE WALKING EYE APP

Your guide now includes a free eBook to your chosen destination,
for the same great price as before. Simply download the Walking Eye
App from the App Store or Google Play to access your free eBook.

HOW THE WALKING EYE APP WORKS

Through the Walking Eye App, you can purchase a range of eBooks and destination
content. However, when you buy this book, you can download the corresponding
eBook for free. Just see below in the grey panel where to find your free content and
then scan the QR code at the bottom of this page.

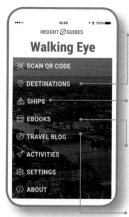

Destinations: Download essential destination
content featuring recommended sights and
attractions, restaurants, hotels and an A–Z of
practical information, all available for purchase.

Ships: Interested in ship reviews? Find
independent reviews of river and ocean ships
in this section, all available for purchase.

eBooks: You can download your free
accompanying digital version of this guide
here. You will also find a whole range of other
eBooks, all available for purchase.

Free access to travel-related blog articles
about different destinations, updated on a
daily basis.

HOW THE EBOOKS WORK

The eBooks are provided in EPUB file format. Please note that you will need an eBook reader installed on your device to open the file. Many devices come with this as standard, but you may still need to install one manually from Google Play.

The eBook content is identical to the content in the printed guide.

HOW TO DOWNLOAD THE WALKING EYE APP

1. Download the Walking Eye App from the App Store or Google Play.
2. Open the app and select the scanning function from the main menu.
3. Scan the QR code on this page – you will then be asked a security question to verify ownership of the book.
4. Once this has been verified, you will see your eBook in the purchased ebook section, where you will be able to download it.

Other destination apps and eBooks are available for purchase separately or are free with the purchase of the Insight Guide book.

TOP 10 ATTRACTIONS

IGREJA MATRIZ
Manueline carving at Monchique's beautiful church. See page 43.

LAGOS
This resort combines a rich history with a busy present. See page 32.

SÃO LOURENÇO DOS MATOS
Exuberant hand-painted *azulejo* tiles decorate this church near Faro. See page 56.

SILVES
This historic town was once a Moorish stronghold. See page 44.

PONTA DA PIEDADE
Take a boat trip to see the impressive cliffs, grottoes and rock stacks. See page 34.

TAVIRA
Soak up the atmosphere of Algarve's most picturesque city. See page 69.

IGREJA DO CARMO
Monks' skulls and bones line the weird and wonderful Chapel of Bones in this Faro church. See page 64.

SAGRES
Enjoy an end-of-the-world feeling at Cabo de São Vicente, Europe's southwesternmost point and explore Algarve off the beaten track. See page 27.

FALÉSIA
Sunbathers and beachcombers will appreciate the charms of this beach east of Albufeira. See page 53.

OLHÃO FISH MARKET
Join the hustle and bustle and see the catch of the day. See page 68.

A PERFECT TOUR

Day 1

Faro

Start your trip in Faro, exploring the Cidade Velha (Old Town), with its fine buildings, Sé (Cathedral) and the Igreja de Nossa Senhora do Carmo and its macabre Capela dos Ossos (Chapel of Bones). Spend the afternoon on Faro's sparkling town beach, the Praia de Faro, with mile upon mile of white sands.

Day 3

Tavira

Travel further along the coast to explore Algarve's loveliest town, Tavira, which straddles the Rio Gilão. Sights include the Renaissance Igreja da Misericórdia, and you can explore the nearby salt pans and take a ferry across to the breathtaking Ilha de Tavira, a long white-sand spit that stretches as far as the eye can see.

Day 4

Algarve interior

Next, head inland to explore the slow-moving, unspoilt interior of the region, which feels like a different world. Visit Silves, a town with slanting red roofs that resembles a Cezanne painting. It is set high above the Rio Arade and topped by a handsome, sandstone castle.

Day 2

Parque Natural da Ria Formosa

Enjoy a delicious seafood lunch in Olhão, Algarve's most workaday, but still handsome, town before heading out to the coastal countryside to explore Parque Natural da Ria Formosa, a beautiful area of lagoons, dunes, beaches and pine forests. You can arrange boat trips through the park from Olhão.

Day 6

Coastal Lagos

Picturesque Lagos is Algarve's most vibrant coastal town, and a great place to base yourself for a few days, enjoying the charming town centre, with sights such as the stunningly baroque Igreja de Santo António, white-and-black paved streets, and lively restaurants and bars.

Day 8

Wild Sagres

Finish off your tour by taking a trip to Sagres, an appropriately grand finale at Algarve's western tip. With its great sea cliffs and views of endless ocean, this is a place unlike anywhere else on the Algarve. Its wild beaches are popular with surfers, there's an imposing clifftop castelo, and the Cabo de São Vicente is the southwesternmost point of mainland Europe.

Day 5

Into the mountains

Travel farther north to discover Algarve's mountain range, the Serra de Monchique. The spa town of Monchique is set amid cool woodlands and is a good place to relax and indulge in some spa treatments at the pastel-hued resort of the Caldas de Monchique.

Day 7

Beach relaxation

Spend your day relaxing on the beaches around Lagos: head for the smaller, more secluded sands found south of the town. You can go sailing, windsurfing and take boat trips, and explore the incredible rock formations along this part of the coast, where ochre cliffs meet searing-blue Atlantic sea.

CONTENTS

INTRODUCTION

For much of the world, Algarve is synonymous with Portugal, yet the Portuguese will tell you the exact opposite: the region has little in common with the rest of the country. The southern stretch of coast is more reminiscent of a North African landscape than a European one. Its towns are small and mostly dedicated to holidaying and fishing; it has no cosmopolitan cities to rival Lisbon and Porto, further north. Most of Portugal is known for quaint towns, medieval castles and grand palaces. Much of, but not all of, Algarve has been colonised by tourist apartments, hotels and golf courses.

The reason for this profusion is the region's coast and climate. Think Algarve and the mind pictures long, glorious stretches of golden sands, secluded coves framed by odd ochre-coloured rock formations, and deep green waters. With about 160km (100 miles) of coastline, Portugal's southern province is one of Europe's premier beach destinations. The occasionally chilly ocean is the Atlantic, but the Algarve has a sultry Mediterranean feel.

SUN, SAND AND SPORTS

The Algarve's temperate weather is the best in Portugal, and one of the kindest in the world: more than 250 days of sunshine a year – more than almost any other resort area. The moderating effect of the Gulf Stream produces a fresh springtime breeze throughout winter, and in late January and February, white almond blossoms blanket the fields. In summer the heat is intense but rarely unbearable, and regardless, beautiful beaches and innumerable pools are always just a drive away.

Magnificent year-round weather has made the Algarve a huge destination for sporting holidays. Superb golf facilities abound – several with tees dramatically clinging to cliffs and fairways just skirting the edge of the ocean – and horse riding, tennis, big-game fishing, sailing and windsurfing are immensely popular.

Sports, beaches and hospitable weather, not to mention the increasing number of low-cost carriers, are surely the reasons that the Algarve receives as many visitors as the rest of Portugal in its entirety. But

The beach at Albufeira

it's not just international tourists that descend on the Algarve: many Portuguese from Lisbon and elsewhere in the north have holiday homes and spend their summer holidays here.

A COASTAL PROVINCE

The coast is neatly divided into the rugged Barlavento to the west and the flat beauty of Sotavento to the east. West is where you'll find the famous orange cliffs and surreal eroded rock stacks. Near Cabo de São Vicente and Sagres, the extreme western point, the terrain is surprisingly barren and the facilities decidedly low-key. The ocean can also be forbiddingly cold.

Tourist resorts cluster along the centre of the coast, from Lagos to Faro, with a spectrum of homes away from home – from monster high-rises to spacious, single-storey villas – spilling across the rolling hills and lining the beaches. Resorts such as Portimão, Albufeira and Vilamoura would appear to have little room left to grow, yet tourist facilities seem to mate with each other and reproduce overnight. Much of the development around these centres is not particularly attractive and resolutely commercial, and these areas get packed out in summer.

The eastern third of the Algarve is a more serene marriage of coast and ocean, with warm waters and hot sands stretching past the wetlands of Ria Formosa to the Spanish border. The Algarve's most picturesque town, Tavira, is along this section of the coast.

Further inland, the terrain slopes through pines, mimosa, eucalyptus and heather to an altitude of nearly 915 metres (3,000ft). Holidaymakers wishing to escape the beach crowds can run for the hills, especially the tantalising Serra de Monchique.

PEOPLE OF THE SEA

The region's exotic name is derived from the Arabic, *Al-Gharb*, meaning 'country of the west'. The westernmost territory of Europe was highly prized by North African Moors, who occupied it from the 8th to the 13th century. Their half millennium here left indelible traces, seen today in whitewashed houses, hill-top castles and colourful ceramic tiles.

Following the recapture of Iberia by Christians, the Algarve led Portugal to glory. Prince Henry the Navigator established his Navigation School along Portugal's southern coast, and intrepid explorers set out in caravels from Lagos and Sagres. In the 15th and 16th centuries, they ushered in an Age of Discovery, rounding Africa's Cape of Good Hope and eventually reaching India and the Pacific. Others found their way to the Americas and Brazil. Opening world trade routes across the globe, they established Portugal as a maritime superpower.

Portugal soon lapsed into decline though, tattered by wars and constitutional crises, and for two centuries or more the

Algarve remained isolated from the rest of Europe. Even though the coast received many illustrious visitors from Roman times through the Middle Ages and up to the Edwardian period (when travellers came to luxuriate in Monchique's spa waters), the Algarve's elite holiday status is a relatively recent phenomenon. The first resort on the coast, Praia da Rocha, was only 'discovered' in the 1930s, and the real build-up didn't kick into overdrive until the early 1980s.

Spain's Costa del Sol developed earlier and more rapidly, yet the lessons of rampant, ill-advised development across the border were not heeded. Only recently has environmental and aesthetic consciousness at least mandated that newer developments are limited in height.

Yet – despite the tourism onslaught – significant parts of the Algarve retain their old-fashioned charm. The main road along the coast, the N125, may be lined with ceramic shops and stifled with summer traffic, but there are some beautiful stretches of beach where you can escape if you explore beyond the main resorts, while the countryside to the north is a different world. Orchards and grain fields replace hotels, apartments and snack bars. A slow, rural lifestyle perseveres against the rush of modern life.

Fishing boats in the port town of Tavira

For centuries, fishing has been the Algarve's lifeblood. Small fishing villages preserve their simple and unaffected ways, seemingly oblivious to the tourist hordes. Scrappy crews of small hand-painted boats troll the waters just offshore, and trawlers fish deep in the Atlantic for *bacalhau* (cod), which is beloved by the Portuguese.

A visit to the local fish market is a revealing window into Algarvian life. Negotiations are serious but friendly. The same scenario is played out at markets all across the region; every town has a market day at least once a month. Farmers bring their livestock to trade, and artisans and vendors sell their wares.

Not large in size, the Algarve is relatively easy to get around, whether by train or car (an effort that is much more relaxing outside of the main summer season). The distances between mega-resorts and unspoiled villages are surprisingly small.

VESTIGES OF THE PAST

Algarve's major attractions, besides beaches, are towns that have lived through centuries of triumph and disaster. Faro, Tavira and Lagos have a strong Moorish influence, and the quiet mountain towns of Silves, Alte and Salir are reminders of Algarve of yesteryear.

Despite the region's ancient roots, few historic monuments survive from before 1755, when Algarve was rocked by a monumental earthquake. Still, you'll find vestiges of a vibrant past, including evocative castle ruins and churches with extraordinary displays of Portuguese glazed tiles. Even the humblest village has a classic white church, a sleepy plaza shaded by vivid purple jacaranda, and, if you time it right, the drama of the local market.

The Portuguese are famously hospitable, if reserved. They remain tolerant and helpful, even though they know that their lovely coast is no longer just theirs.

A BRIEF HISTORY

Little is known of the earliest Stone Age inhabitants of Europe's southwestern extremity. The ancient Greeks called them the Cynetes (or Cunetes). Whatever their origins, their culture evolved under the pressure and influence of foreign forces. Among the many invading armies that settled here and contributed to nascent Portuguese culture were Phoenicians, who settled in the area around 1000 BC, followed by the Celts, Iberians, Greeks and Carthaginians.

But it was the Romans, who arrived late in the 3rd century BC, who most greatly influenced Iberia. They built towns, roads and bridges, developed industries and agriculture, and bequeathed the Latin language, of which Portuguese is a descendant. The Romans named the southwestern province of the peninsula Lusitania, after one of the Celtiberian tribes they had defeated, and by the 3rd century AD had introduced Christianity. By the early 4th century the Algarve had a bishop in place, based in Faro. But Rome had fallen into decay, and soon hordes of northern tribesmen took over the empire. The Algarve fell to the Visigoths in the mid-5th century.

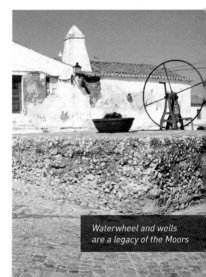

Waterwheel and wells are a legacy of the Moors

UNDER MOORISH RULE

In AD 711, the Moors brought powerful armies from North Africa and launched a devastating attack on the Iberian peninsula, conquering much of what would become Spain and Portugal. They imposed Islam and left an indelible influence on the countryside and population of the Algarve. The Moorish legacy can still be seen in the form of wells and waterwheels, squat white houses, the dark complexions of the people and in the very name of the region – taken from *Al-Gharb*, which means 'country of the west' (when the Moors conquered the territory, it was the most westerly in the known world).

The Moors governed their Iberian kingdoms from across the border in Seville, but the Algarve had its own regional capital and huge, invulnerable fortress. The capital was Chelb (or Xelb),

Silves was the capital of Algarve under the Moors

and it was bigger and better defended than Lisbon. Today the town, known as Silves (see page 44), is a provincial outpost whose only besiegers are busloads of tourists.

The struggle by Christians to expel the Moors (a campaign known as the *Reconquista*, or Reconquest) began in the late 8th century AD. By the 11th century, Portucale consisted of a small section of territory previously held by Castile and León (which became today's northern Portugal). Yet it wasn't until the 12th century that significant gains were made to take back southern Iberia. The beginning of the end came in the Battle of Ourique in 1139. After the victory, Count Afonso Henriques proclaimed himself the first king of Portugal, making it one of the first nation-states in Europe.

The Reconquest of Silves, not achieved for another 50 years, was a grisly affair. A mixed bag of Crusaders from northern Europe were recruited en route to their battles east in the Holy Land. They sailed upon the river port of Silves and, ignoring conditional offers of surrender, slew all the inhabitants (at no small loss to themselves) and pillaged the great treasures of the city.

Two years later Muslim forces rallied again, retaking Silves, and the *Reconquista* stumbled on for another half century. So many inter-religious alliances reigned, and so pervasive was the intermingling of Moors and Christians, that it was hard to tell who was on which side and for which piece of land they were fighting. The situation was further clouded by a feud between Portugal and Spain, each of them claiming sovereignty over the Algarve. However, by 1249 Faro and the western Algarve were retaken under King Afonso III, completing the *Reconquista*. The possibility of war with Spain was averted by an expeditious royal marriage, and at the century's close a treaty with Spain drew up the boundaries of Portugal that stand today.

The Algarve was a region regarded separately within the new Portugal, as is evidenced by the royal title 'Kingdom of Portugal and the Algarve'. In those days, the notion of the Algarve as a distinct entity did make some sense: like an island, it was cut off to the south and west by the Atlantic, to the east by the Guadiana River, and to the north by the Serra de Monchique mountain range. The region's titular autonomy was upheld until 1910, when the monarchy itself was overthrown.

A tribute to Henry in Lagos

HENRY THE NAVIGATOR

In 1415, long after the *Reconquista* was completed, a Portuguese fleet assembled on the River Tagus in Lisbon, ready for an assault on the Moors in their homeland. Crossing the Straits of Gibraltar, the armada attacked and seized the North African city of Ceuta. An illustrious member of the famous raid was the young Prince Henry – half Portuguese and half English – and the son of King João I and his wife, Philippa of Lancaster. Ceuta would be Henry's one and only military victory, though he was destined to establish Portugal as a major world power, helping to develop important world trade routes by the time of his death in 1460.

The waters at the western extreme of the Algarve were all that was known to sailors. Once they were beyond Cabo de São Vicente, they faced the unknown, with no communications and no possibility of rescue if the voyage turned out badly. Yet out into the unknown they went; for the glory of God and country, and in search of personal fame and fortune. Their mission was made easier by the craft Algarve shipwrights had developed, a successor to the lumbering ships of the day: the caravel. It was light, fast and very manoeuvrable. With the subsequent development of new navigational techniques, it was no longer necessary to stay within sight of land. Now the only limits to maritime exploration were man's ingenuity and courage.

During Henry's lifetime, Portugal's caravels sailed beyond the most westerly point of Africa. They colonised the Atlantic islands of Madeira and the Azores, laying the foundations for the future Portuguese Empire. Before the century was over, Henry's compatriots Bartolomeu Dias and Vasco da Gama both completed epic voyages, rounding the Cape of Good Hope and reaching India respectively, and Pedro Álves Cabral claimed Brazil. Between 1519 and 1522 another Portuguese explorer, Ferdinand Magellan, led the first expedition to circumnavigate the world. Mercantilist Portugal became a rich maritime superpower.

FOREIGN INTRIGUES

To protect its seagoing interests and trade routes, Portugal established strategic garrisons in Goa (India), Malacca (East Indies) and Hormuz in the Persian Gulf. Portuguese explorers

⊙ SCHOOL OF NAVIGATION

At the age of 21, Henry assembled a School of Navigation. It was certainly not a formal institution of lectures and classes, but probably resembled an informal modern-day 'think-tank'. Prince Henry – made governor of the Algarve in 1418 – had the money, influence, enthusiasm and vision to lead and cajole the best astronomers, cartographers, boat-designers and seamen of the day to expand Portugal's maritime horizons.

According to tradition, the site of Prince Henry's base was the Sagres peninsula (see page 27), though there is little there today to persuade you of this. The actual headquarters of the Navigation School may have been 40km (25 miles) east, in Lagos (see page 32). This location had a port and shipyards, and was home to the prince in his role as governor of the Algarve.

Beyond the grave

For many years after his death, legends and rumours bizarrely insisted that King Sebastião was still alive, and imposters turned up from time to time claiming the throne; those who were plausible enough to be deemed a threat were summarily executed.

then embarked upon Macau (now Macao), the Congo and various other parts of Africa, including the Sudan. The Portuguese policy was to avoid armed strife and to develop a trade empire, rather than to conquer nations. To this end it succeeded with relatively few blood-soaked episodes in its colonial history.

Adventures abroad, however, proved disastrous during the second half of the 16th century. In 1557 the 14-year-old boy-king Sebastião ascended the throne, the beginning of a calamitous reign that was to end at the battle of Alcacer-Quiber (Morocco) in pursuit of a vain crusade. Sebastião's untimely demise, alongside some 18,000 ill-prepared, badly led followers, set the stage for a crisis of succession.

The only rightful claimant to the crown was an elderly prince, Henry. But after two years of alternating between the throne and his sickbed, he died, heirless. Spain, sensing an opportunity, occupied the power vacuum, and Portugal's neighbour and long-time antagonist became its master.

Spanish rule dictated Portugal's inadvertent involvement in Spain's ongoing wars. In 1587 a squadron of English ships commanded by Francis Drake attacked the Algarve (now a 'legitimate target' as Spanish territory) and sacked Sagres, thus depriving the world of the relics of Henry the Navigator. Nine years later Faro was torched by command of the Earl of Essex. The 1386 Treaty of Windsor, by which England and Portugal had pledged eternal friendship, seemed a distant memory.

Portugal's empire was gradually eroded, and many of its trading posts (with the exception of Brazil) were picked off by the English and Dutch. Finally, after 60 years of Spanish rule, Portuguese noblemen (aided by the French, then at war with Spain) organised a palace coup and restored independence in 1640.

THE GREAT DISASTER

Portugal's greatest misfortune struck on All Saints' Day, 1 November 1755. With candlelit churches crowded with worshippers, an earthquake struck, followed by fast-spreading fires and a devastating tidal wave that swept over the Algarve as far as 6.5km (4 miles) inland. The exact casualty figure will never be known, but it is estimated that 5,000 died immediately and between 40,000 and 60,000 perished as a result of secondary

The effects of the earthquake were felt as far away as Lisbon

injuries and the ensuing famine and pestilence. The epicentre of the earthquake is thought to have been off the Algarve coast, possibly between Tavira and Faro, but it devastated places as far away as the capital, Lisbon.

Throughout the Algarve and much of the rest of southern Portugal, virtually every important monument, cathedral, castle and mansion was destroyed, or at least critically damaged in the earthquake. Among the hardest-hit towns was Lagos (see page 32) which lost its castle, its churches and the palace in which Henry the Navigator had once lived.

POLITICAL UPHEAVAL

The beginning of the 19th century brought further alarm. This time the epicentre was Paris, and the cause of the problems, Napoleon. Just as Portugal's forced alliance with Spain had made the country a target for Drake's 16th-century raids, now her friendly alliance with Britain rankled Napoleon.

In 1807 the French invaded Lisbon, causing the royal family to flee to Brazil. Spain, followed by Portugal, rose up against the French occupation, in what came to be known as the Peninsular War. Among the early blows struck for independence was a rebellion in the town of Olhão (see page 65).

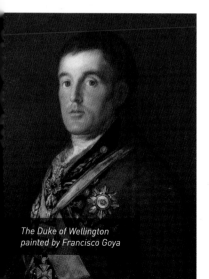

The Duke of Wellington painted by Francisco Goya

On 16 June 1808, the townsfolk – armed with little more than ancient swords, spears and stones – attacked and captured the local French garrison. The real battle, however, was waged under the leadership of the Duke of Wellington, whose coalition forces expelled the French after two years of bitter fighting.

The war left Portugal further weakened, and in 1822 its major empire outpost, Brazil, declared independence. At the same time, a dispute over the crown continually raged between Pedro IV, the absentee monarch who preferred to reign as Emperor of Brazil rather than return to Portugal, and his brother Miguel. The power struggle excited the interest of other nations. With British help, Pedro defeated Miguel off Cape St Vincent in 1833, and his expeditionary force marched to Lisbon. Pedro took the throne, though armed struggle continued for months.

By 1892 Portugal, racked by wars and the continuing expense of maintaining its African colonies (including those of Mozambique and Angola), declared itself bankrupt. The seeds of discontent with absolutist rule were sown.

KINGDOM'S END

On 1 February 1908, the royal family was riding in an open carriage along the Lisbon riverfront plaza when an assassin opened fire, killing King Carlos and the heir to the throne, Prince Luis Filipe. The prince's younger brother, Prince Manuel, was also hit, but survived and was thus propelled to the throne at the tender age of 19. Amid republican agitation, a surprise uprising led by elements within the armed forces deposed Manuel in 1910.

The sudden end of more than seven centuries of monarchy brought confusion. Presidents and prime ministers were ushered into and out of office an unbelievable 45 times between 1910 and 1926, until a military revolution suspended Portugal's problematic democracy. After six years of power, General Oscar Carmona appointed his finance minister, António de Oliveira Salazar, to be prime minister, a position he was to hold until 1968. Salazar's repressive rule and austerity measures rid the Portuguese economy of debt, though poverty increased. Portugal remained neutral during World War II, and Salazar demonstrated his financial acumen by selling materials and supplies to both sides.

In 1968 the elderly Salazar was forced into retirement after a stroke. His successor, Dr Marcelo Caetano, feeling the spirit of the age, began tentative relaxations of the old regime. The armed forces finally overthrew him in a popular bloodless coup, known as the 'Carnation Revolution', on 25 April 1974.

Portugal finally began to pull itself out of the long and fruitless struggle against revolutionaries in its African colonies, and granted independence to the remaining members of its empire in 1975.

In 1986 Portugal, the former poor backwater of Europe, joined the European Economic Community (now the European Union, or EU). With EU aid, Portugal became one of the fastest-growing countries in Europe. The Algarve, already a favourite of sun-seeking beach lovers, benefited from EU funds to build up its infrastructure and to invest in tourism.

In 2008 the global financial crisis brought new economic hardship. Forced to accept a €78-billion EU bailout in 2011 and introduce a drastic austerity programme, the economy slowly recovered, and the government finally exited the bailout programme in 2014. With the Portuguese economy registering 1.3 percent growth in 2015, the centre-left cabinet, led by Prime Minister Antonio Costa, hinted that austerity measures could be relaxed. The country received another boost of optimism when the national football squad won the Euro 2016 in France.

Tourism in the Algarve continues to flourish – despite violent wildfires hitting the region in 2016 – with a record 3.7-million visitors in 2015.

HISTORICAL LANDMARKS

c. 1000BC Phoenicians settle in the Algarve region.

700BC Celtic tribes arrive.

205BC Romans create Lusitania province.

5th century Algarve falls to the Visigoths.

711 Moors arrive on the Iberian peninsula and swiftly conquer it.

883 Northern Portugal (Portucale) regained by Christian forces.

1139 Count Afonso Henriques declares himself first king of Portugal.

1249 Moors are finally expelled from Algarve.

1415 The Atlantic island of Madeira reached by explorers under the patronage of Henry the Navigator, starting the Age of Discoveries.

1498 Vasco da Gama opens a sea route to India.

1500 Pedro Álvares Cabral reaches Brazil.

1580 Portugal falls under Spanish rule for 60 years.

1587 English fleet sacks Sagres.

1755 The Great Earthquake devastates the Algarve, as well as Lisbon.

1807 Napoleonic troops invade Portugal at the start of the Peninsular War; royal family leaves for Brazil.

1829–34 Civil war between Pedro IV and Miguel I.

1892 Portugal declares itself bankrupt.

1908 King Carlos I and Prince Luis Filipe assassinated.

1910 Monarchy overthrown; Portugal becomes a republic.

1932 António de Salazar becomes prime minister and effective dictator.

1974 The Carnation Revolution restores democracy; Portugal pulls out of African colonies and a million expatriates return.

1986 Portugal joins the European Economic Community (now the EU).

1999 Macau, Portugal's last remaining colony, is returned to the Chinese.

2002 The euro replaces the escudo as the national currency.

2011 Portugal becomes the third EU country to ask for a bailout.

2013 The economy slowly picks up after three years of recession.

2015 Antonio Costa's new centre-left cabinet promises to relax austerity measures.

2016 Forest fires ravage large swathes of Algarve and Madeira.

Picturesque rock formations at Praia de Três Irmãos

 WHERE TO GO

The Algarve stretches from the Atlantic Ocean to Spain, but it's actually a small region. Faro, the capital, is just 50km (30 miles) from the Spanish border, and it is only 112km (70 miles) west of what was known in medieval times as *o fim do mundo* (the end of the world) at Sagres. Along this 160km (100-mile) coastal strip, resorts and holiday villages of all types have sprung up, so wherever you are based, you'll never be far from a good beach, a reasonably sized town, village, or resort, shops and nightlife.

The following pages cover the Algarve from west to east, though you could of course do the reverse or begin in the centre, in or around Faro, and embark on day trips both east and west from there. The A22 motorway, or IP1 (toll payable), provides fast access across the region, running north of the slow-going, but toll-free, coastal N125. For those with additional time and an interest in seeing the Portuguese capital, a brief section on Lisbon is included. Lisbon is about two to three hours by train or car (and 40 minutes by plane) from Faro; it should be conceived of as an add-on to your visit to the Algarve rather than a day trip.

WESTERN ALGARVE

THE SAGRES PENINSULA

If you begin your journey at **Sagres ❶**, you'll be in for a surprise. Rather than the built-up tourist resorts the Algarve is famous for, it has a remote, rugged, undiscovered feel. There is only a relative smattering of hotels, restaurants and other facilities aimed at tourists here, making it like an outpost of the Algarve – which is precisely why it has so many admirers. In particular, it is favoured by surfers.

Sagres' connections to the sea are strong. Prince Henry the Navigator established his Navigation School here (though some suggest that it was further east, near Lagos). The town has a picturesque working harbour, where small, brightly painted fishing boats bob and larger vessels haul in daily catches of lobster, eel and mackerel. A couple of restaurants are clustered around the harbour, with impressive views. Inland, a cute little square, Praça República, is ringed by informal (and, in summer, heaving) nightspots.

The best beaches near Sagres are sheltered and not over-crowded. **Mareta**, down below the *pousada* (government-owned inn), is the most popular. **Martinhal**, just east of the harbour,

The rocky peninsula near Sagres

is a wide, curved beach. **Beliche** (also written Belixe) is a sandy expanse protected by the Cabo de São Vicente. **Tonel**, just before Beliche, and **Telheiro**, about 9km (6 miles) up the west coast from Sagres, are also well-regarded beach spots. There are plenty of companies offering watersports in this area, particularly surfing.

Henry's Sagres

Henry the Navigator – Infante Dom Henrique – was bequeathed the land around Sagres in 1443 by his brother. Henry lived within the castle and died in Sagres in 1460, though his remains were later transferred to the Batalha monastery north of Lisbon.

Beyond the village of Sagres, a great, rocky peninsula hangs above a brooding ocean. You'll understand why, in the days before the great Portuguese explorers set out from here seeking to discover the great beyond, it was known as the End of the World. Those wishing to put a positive spin on things called it Sacrum Saturni – Holy Promontory – and believed that the gods slept here.

Since time immemorial this forlorn place has stirred the imagination. Henry and his sailors are said to have set up camp at the **Fortaleza de Sagres** (Fortress; daily May–Sept 9.30am–8pm, Oct–Apr 9.30am–5.30pm; free 1st Sun of month) that fills the promontory. Unfortunately, not much of the original has survived. Most of it is a 17th-century fort that was insensitively restored: the walls have been resurfaced with grey concrete and whitewashed, masking the external character of the building, though it still has an imposing, wind-buffeted appeal. The fortress's principal building, which may have been Henry's headquarters, no longer exists. What you'll find inside is a small 16th-century chapel, Nossa Senhora da Graça, and what looks to be a huge stone sundial, known as the **Rosa dos**

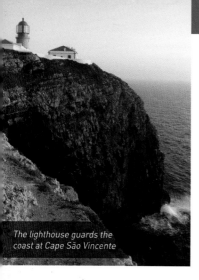
The lighthouse guards the coast at Cape São Vincente

Ventos (Rose Compass). A modern hall on the fort's grounds houses an exhibition area with a rewarding view over the coastline.

A couple of kilometres (1 mile) west of Sagres are the more authentic remains of another fortress, **Fortaleza do Beliche**. This small and attractive 17th-century castle houses a white, domed chapel (Santa Catarina). Both the fort and chapel, however, threaten to collapse because the surrounding cliffs are eroding at a frightening rate and the site, at one time a hotel, is now considered dangerous and off-limits.

The windswept cliffs of **Cabo de São Vicente**, the most southwesterly point in Europe, were once surely even more bleak than they are today, when supertankers and small yachts heave into view. But even on the calmest of days, the Atlantic thunders below and the wind whips around the cape. At the tip of the point, the lighthouse, built in 1904 on the site of a convent chapel, has a beam visible up to 96km (60 miles) away. Visitors can climb the stairs to a hot, enclosed lookout (Wed summer 2–5pm, winter 1.30–4.30pm; free).

The first settlement of any size outside Sagres is **Vila do Bispo**, situated 7km (4 miles) to the north. Take a break in the peaceful town's pleasant, flower-filled garden square and pay a visit to the 18th-century parish church. The walls are covered with *azulejos* (tiles) and the ceiling decorated with frescoes.

About halfway between Sagres and Lagos, **Salema** is a nicely small-scale, laidback resort, popular with independent travellers, with a lively sprinkling of bars and restaurants, and a lovely wide sandy beach.

Burgau, 3.2km (2 miles) east, is small and sleepy, though it gets busy in July and August. It has another appealing sandy beach, backed by craggy cliffs, with the road down to it lined by fishing boats. The small village retains its easy-going local character.

Luz is a pleasant seaside town, another low-key, attractive small resort. All that remains of old Luz is the church and, opposite, the **fortress**, which has been renovated and converted into a restaurant (www.fortalezadaluz.com). There is a good beach with watersport facilities and large, flat rocks for sunbathing.

Avenida dos Descobrimentos in Lagos

LAGOS

The principal resort of the western Algarve, **Lagos** ❷ is the rare beach town that offers something for everyone. By night Lagos is lively, with outdoor restaurant terraces and bars attracting a hipper crowd than most resorts on the coast, and by day it combines a rich historical past with a busy present. Attractive beaches are just on the outskirts of town, so it is not a classic resort in the style of Praia da Rocha.

Your first view of Lagos will probably be from the long, riverside Avenida dos Descobrimentos, which divides the old walled city from the port. At the other end of the avenue, the well-restored fortress, **Forte da Ponte da Bandeira** ❹, guarded the entrance to the harbour in the 17th century. Cross the river to see busy fishermen, handsome boats anchored in the marina and the fine view of the city above the walls. Many of the streets rising towards the top of town are narrow, cobbled and more accustomed to donkeys than rental cars. Though Lagos town still retains a good part of its original walls – most of them from the 16th century but part-Roman in places – they have been rebuilt and expanded over the centuries. Climb the ramparts for fine views over the port and out to sea.

Lagos was an important trading port under the Moors, but the town enjoyed its heyday after the Christian Reconquest. It was proclaimed the capital of the Algarve, and the governor's palace became the headquarters of Prince Henry. A formal statue of Henry, seated with sextant in hand, has been erected on Praça Dom Henrique next to the main avenue. Arguments persist over the exact whereabouts of the prince's School of Navigation, but it seems almost certain that Lagos was the principal shipyard and port serving his team of explorers.

Those were the glory years, but there was a dark side to all this. Explorations along the west coast of Africa in the

Lagos' old city walls

mid-15th century established a flourishing slave trade, and Lagos was a key player in human commerce. Just behind the statue of Henry, on the corner of Rua da Senhora da Graça, you can still see the small arcade where Portugal's first slave auctions took place. A small plaque states simply **Mercado de Escravos** (Slave Market). Most other historic buildings around the square succumbed to the devastating earthquake of 1755 (see page 21). The majority of the city's attractive buildings thus date from the late 18th and 19th centuries.

On Rua General Alberta da Silveira, the tiny **Igreja de Santo António** , an exuberant gilt baroque work and one of the Algarve's finest churches, was rebuilt soon after the earthquake. The church, a national monument dedicated to St Anthony, has a handsome display of 18th-century blue-and-white glazed tiles and a brightly painted wooden ceiling. Set into the floor you'll find the tomb of an Irish colonel,

Hugh Beatty, a soldier of fortune who commanded the Lagos Regiment of the Portuguese Army in the late 18th century, and who must have been held in very high esteem to have been awarded such a prestigious final resting place.

The entrance to the church is through the curious and eclectic museum next door, the **Museu Municipal D** (Tue–Sun 10am–12.30pm, 2–5.30pm; tel: 282-762 301). Rooms display an array of oddments, including sacred art, archaeological remains, the original charter of Lagos, and holy vestments.

The main street of Lagos is the charming, cobbled **Rua 25 de Abril E**, packed with restaurants, bars and antiques and ceramics shops. The side streets hold some good art and craft galleries and plenty of rewards for exploration. The square at the end of 25 de Abril holds a curious statue, which some liken to an extra-terrestrial, of the boy-king Sebastião. In 1568 Sebastião became king of Portugal at the age of 14. A decade later he embarked on a disastrous voyage to Morocco to fight the Moors. At least 7,000 troops died, the king included.

THE COAST AROUND LAGOS

The beaches near Lagos range from **Meia Praia**, 1.6km (1 mile) to the east, a long (4km/2.5-mile) flat stretch, to pocket-sized coves just west of the city. Weird and wonderful rock formations, and steep cliffs that glow orange at sunset, have made them some of the most photographed in Europe; head for **Praia de Dona Ana** and **Praia do Camilo**, both small, pretty and crowded.

At the southern tip, just before it turns west to Sagres, are the coast's most spectacular sights. **Ponta da Piedade 3** (Point of Piety) is the mother of all stack and cliff formations along the Algarve, a stunning terracotta family of bridges, terraces and grottoes. There is no beach here, but there are great views from above, and in season (spring to autumn) boat trips depart from the foot of the steps that have been cut deep into the sides of the cliff.

NORTHWEST OF LAGOS

For a complete change of scene, take a drive northwest towards the hills and **Bensafrim** ❹. Here you can enjoy the Algarve of yesteryear and rolling undeveloped countryside, where people still live off the land. The tilled soil, a startling ochre colour, makes a bright backdrop for orange and lemon groves. Turn off towards the **Barragem da Bravura** and you'll be rewarded with a sight every bit as inspiring as its name. This body of water, more akin to the English Lake District than sunny southern Europe, is of great practical use, irrigating crops, including rice, around Lagos.

Spectacular rock shapes at the Ponta da Piedade

Colégio dos Jesuítas, Portimão

PORTIMÃO

Second in size only to Faro in the Algarve, **Portimão** ❺ is the most workman-like town on the coast. But nestled around it are some of the Algarve's finest beaches, a fact which has transformed the town into one of the coast's most popular resorts. Praia da Rocha and Praia Três Irmãos in particular are lined with hotels. Most holidaymakers stay along this stretch.

Portimão sits at the confluence of the River Adade and the sea, and most of its local colour is down by the port, a haven of fishing activity. The top fish-canning spot on the Algarve, Portimão is renowned for its restaurants specialising in *sardinhas grelhadas* (grilled sardines). Though Portimão was settled by the Romans, it was one of the Algarve towns most damaged by the earthquake of 1755, and as a consequence has few buildings or monuments of historical interest. **Largo 1° de Dezembro** is a 19th-century addition, a park with 10 splendid blue-and-white *azulejo* benches, each illustrating a pivotal event in the history of Portugal. The park's name alludes to the date, 1 December 1640, when Portugal's independence from Spain was restored (see page 21).

Much of the town centre is pedestrian-only and filled with shops. The main square, at Rua do Comércio and Avenida São João de Deus, is where you'll find the large and austere

Colégio dos Jesuítas (Jesuit College). The church, constructed at the end of the 17th century, is the largest on the Algarve.

Around the corner, along Rua Machado dos Santos, is the handsome **Igreja de Nossa Senhora da Conceição**, sitting atop a small hill and incline of steps. The yellow-and-white church, originally constructed in the 15th century, has a beautiful Gothic portico with carved capitals, but looks like a colonial church you might find in Brazil, due to its reconstruction and remodelling during the 18th and 19th centuries.

From the centre of town, head to the waterfront, especially if it's anywhere near time for lunch or dinner. You can almost follow your nose towards the heady aroma of grilled sardines. It will take you to the **dockside**, which is lined with simple restaurants, one after the other, all serving delicious, smoky sardines (and other freshly caught fish). Choose whichever spot seems to be bustling with ravenous patrons. A plate of grilled sardines, prawns or squid and a bottle of house wine make a fantastic meal, and the prices are about as low as anywhere along the coast.

The hectic operations of the fishing industry used to take place here right under the noses of holidaymakers, with a frenetic 'bucket-brigade' hauling wicker baskets of fresh fish up from the boat holds to ice trays and waiting trucks, right next to dockside dining tables. The fishermen were moved to a larger location on the other side of the river, but most sightseeing boats that tour the harbour and nearby grottoes include a quick trip to the new docks. You will still see fishing boats at anchor on the main quay, but the majority of river traffic here now is made up of private yachts, replica sailing ships on tourist excursions and tiny dinghies.

The award-winning **Museu de Portimão** (www.museudeporti mao.pt; Sept–July Tue 2.30–6pm, Wed–Sun 10am–6pm, Aug Tue

7.30–11pm, Wed–Sun 3–11pm) is housed in a former sardine-canning factory, and vividly recreates the factory's former processes, as well as displaying local underwater archaeological finds.

Portimão's other claim to fame is its status as a comprehensive regional shopping centre. There is certainly a good variety of shops here, with several shopping malls as well as outlets selling traditional crafts or locally made items. A market – mainly selling foodstuffs – is often set up in the square opposite the Colégio dos Jesuítas.

PRAIA DA ROCHA

Just 3km (2 miles) down river from Portimão is **Praia da Rocha** ❻, which became a holiday village for wealthy Portuguese

⊙ FISHY BUSINESS

At night out on the ocean, a couple of kilometres or so beyond the beach, you may see tiny specks of light glinting below the stars. These are the lanterns of a small fleet of fishing boats in a wide formation, luring fish into an elaborate net. For centuries fishing has been big business in Algarve, but the biggest boom began 100 years ago when the canning industry came to the region. To this day, thousands of tonnes of fish, mostly sardines, with tuna coming in a close second, are caught, tinned and exported annually.

Those who have tasted plump and juicy sardines fresh from the quay at Portimão or elsewhere in the Algarve – they're best in summer, when mature – can only feel a little sorry for those who have to take their pleasures many weeks later, from a tin. If you're in Portimão during August, check out the Sardine Festival.

The much-photographed beach at Praia da Rocha

families at the end of the 19th century. It was 'discovered' by the British in the 1930s, when this 'beach of rocks', strewn with extravagantly shaped eroded stacks, provided an inspirational refuge for writers and intellectuals. The belle-époque Hotel Bela Vista (www.hotelbelavista.net) is a surviving monument from those days.

Today the 2km (1.3-mile) long golden **beach** is still the main attraction, but the once-small village fronting the beach has been swamped by a sea of hotels and tourist facilities. The sprawl has entirely blurred Praia da Rocha's separate identity from Portimão.

At the far eastern end of the resort, guarding the River Arade, is the **Fortaleza de Santa Catarina de Ribamar** (St Catherine's Fortress), built in 1621 to defend Silves and Portimão against the Moors. Little remains of the actual fortress, but its courtyard is now an agreeable terrace offering fine views out to sea. Directly across from the fort is the splendid **Fortaleza de Ferragudo**, which looks like a giant sandcastle; note that this is closed to the public.

The old fishing village of **Ferragudo** nearby is well worth a visit. Despite its proximity to a main tourist enclave, and two excellent beaches of its own, it has resisted blatant commercialisation, remaining a traditional fishermen's settlement. The opposite end of Praia da Rocha's long stretch is known as **Praia do Vau**. The splendid rock formations and coves continue, but this end of the beach is quieter and less developed than the eastern end.

Just west, **Praia de Três Irmãos** is the slightly upscale beach cousin of Praia da Rocha. Its newest attraction, opened in 2012, is the **Ocean Revival Underwater Park** (www.oceanrevival.

Fishing boats and yachts in Alvor harbour

org). The largest artificial reef in the world, the park is an excellent destination for divers who can explore four sunken warships and marvel at the diverse marine life. The eastern end of the beach is a beautiful cove, hemmed in by cliffs and ochre-coloured rocks. Beyond it, the beach stretches to **Alvor**, a classic Algarvian fishermen's village. Narrow cobbled streets plunge downhill to a quay and market where

The Serra de Monchique

boats bob at anchor on a wide, marshy lagoon. A handful of bars rustle up barbecued sardines. At the top of the hill, on Rua da Igreja, is Igreja Matriz, a delightful 16th-century church, with a delicately carved Manueline portico, perhaps the finest on the Algarve, and excellent 18th-century *azulejos* in the chancel. The large white-sand Praia de Alvor is backed by restaurants, cafe-bars and a great new boardwalk, and close by is the main focus of a recreational area that includes a golf course and a casino.

Between Alvor and the N125, the main coastal road, are the **ruins of Abicada**, a Roman village that dates back to the 4th century AD.

SERRA DE MONCHIQUE

North of Portimão, and extending across the western half of the province, is the Serra de Monchique, a mountain range that protects the coast from the hot plains further north. The *serra* is a verdant landscape of cork, pine and chestnut trees and low-lying areas are covered in wildflowers. Its highest point is Fóia.

Two spots in the *serra* popular with visitors are the villages of Monchique and Caldas de Monchique. The first stop on the scenic journey along route N266 is the spa village of **Caldas de Monchique ❼**, known since Roman times for its therapeutic waters. Its heyday was the Edwardian era, and many of the elegant buildings (including a casino and a handicrafts market) still date from this period. A good place for a picnic and a stroll in the woods, an air of nostalgia has long presided over this sleepy hollow, but renovations have brought the resort into the 21st century. The Monchique Spa (www.monchiquetermas.com), complete with hotels, restaurants and craft shops, offers various treatments, all making use of the mineral-rich waters for which the resort is famed. The water is bottled here and sold across the Algarve.

⊘ THE MANUELINE STYLE

During the reign of Manuel I (1495–1521), artists were inspired as never before by the discovery of far-off lands and the romance of daring sea voyages. The style they evolved, called Manueline after their king, celebrated this brave new age of maritime travel. Motifs such as anchors, knotted ropes, sails, terrestrial globes, marine plants and animals became the signatures of this period's sculptors and architects. In the 16th century, the style fell out of favour and by 1540 Portugal had joined with the rest of Europe in building in the more sober Renaissance style.

The most famous example of Manueline art is Lisbon's Belém Tower, but you can also see exuberant stonework all over the Algarve. Look out for the church portals and windows at Silves (the Igreja da Misericórdia), Alvor, and particularly at Monchique.

To the north of Caldas, the road starts to weave uphill quickly, rising some 300 metres (1,000ft) in 5km (3 miles) past terraced farmlands and forests of eucalyptus, oak and cork. **Monchique 8** is a small market town, known for its handicrafts and the famous Manueline portico of its 16th-century **Igreja Matriz**. The beautiful, unusual church has Romanesque arches, stone columns, blue-and-yellow *azulejos*

The famous Manueline portico of Monchique's Igreja Matriz

(tiles) and a handsome wood ceiling. If you wander around the town, you'll probably see artisans crafting shoes and carving out walking sticks in small workshops in the backstreets.

High above the town, the ruins of a 17th-century Franciscan monastery, **Nossa Senhora do Desterro**, loom like a ghostly grey eminence. A visit here will be rewarded by a breathtaking view, and a beautiful walk through ancient woodland.

The road continues upwards, passing roadside souvenir stalls and fruit vendors and a few well-placed restaurants. At the end of the line is **Fóia**, almost 915 metres (3,000ft) above sea level, affording one of the best views in southern Portugal. There is no settlement here, just a collection of craft and souvenir stalls, a bar, a restaurant, TV masts and an obelisk marking the highest point on the Algarve. On a clear day you can see from the bay of Portimão to the Sagres peninsula and pick out the rocky outcrops of the Lagos beaches.

The Moorish castle and Christian cathedral dominate the city of Silves

Although you may welcome the breeze after the heat of the coast, the wind blows pretty briskly at Fóia, so you'll need a jacket or sweater.

SILVES

Back down the main road towards Portimão, a turn-off to **Silves ❾** leads to the former Moorish capital of the Algarve. More than eight centuries ago, Silves (then known as Chelb) was a magnificent city with palaces, gardens, bazaars and a huge red castle on a hill. Granada in Spain has the Alhambra, the legendary palace of the Moors, but the Algarve also possesses a city straight out of *Arabian Nights*.

The golden age of Silves began in AD 711 with the Muslim invasion. With redoubtable fortifications and a population in the tens of thousands, it was one of the strongest outposts in 12th-century Arab Iberia. The Crusaders attacked and took the city in 1189, only to see it recovered by the Moors two years later. A half-decade later, the Christians captured Silves for good. However, the loss of Arabic wealth and the silting up of the River Arade left Silves almost literally high and dry, and by the time the bishopric of the Algarve was transferred to Faro in 1577 the town's population had dwindled to 140.

Its riches were stolen long ago, the once-great river is a silted shadow of its former self, and Silves is now just a dusty backwater; but the glorious setting and parts of the evocative old town remain. Surmounted by its red fortress, Silves climbs the hillside from the river, its medieval bridge still intact. The old city inside the gates still evokes the layout of the Jewish quarter and *almedina* of the Moors.

Though a castle of sorts has existed here since Phoenician times, the present structure, known as **de Silves** (tel: 282 440 837; daily June–Sept 9am–11pm, Oct–May 9am–5.30pm), on the site of Roman or Visigothic foundations, took shape after the Christian Reconquest, though it preserves distinctly Moorish lines. Oleander and jacaranda soften its bellicose nature, and there are fine views over the tiled roofs of the town and surrounding countryside. A

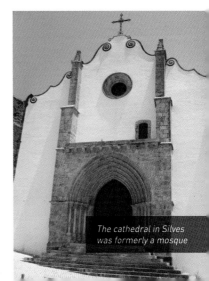

The cathedral in Silves was formerly a mosque

long-destroyed 'Palace of Verandas' once existed within the castle; today you can see only a deep well (60 metres/200ft).

Next to the castle is the impressive Gothic **Sé Velha** (Old Cathedral) of Silves, built in the 13th century by the liberating Crusaders, some of whom are buried within. The remains of a Moorish mosque are hidden behind the altar. Opposite the Sé is the 16th-century **Igreja da Misericórdia**, with a classic Manueline-style side door.

Wander down to the main square, the Praça do Municipio. The imposing **Torreão da Porta da Cidade** (Turret of the City Gate) gives you a good idea of how seriously defence of the city was taken. This sturdy, war-like structure now houses the peaceful municipal library (open to the public). Close by, on Rua das Portas de Loulé, is an impressive **Museu Municipal de Arqueologia** (archaeology museum; daily 10am–6pm). Here you can see part of a large Arab water cistern and other local finds.

The hills around Silves form a prosperous farming region; figs, oranges, lemons, grapefruit, clementines and pomegranates are all grown in abundance in vast stretches of orchards.

Just outside the city, on the road to São Bartolomeu de Messines (route N124), is an important 16th-century religious sculpture. Known as the **Cruz de Portugal** (Cross of Portugal), it depicts the crucifixion of Christ on one face and the descent from the cross on the other.

If you are travelling by car, continue to the **Barragem** (dam) **do Arade**. The water collected in this reservoir surrounded by pine hills provides irrigation for the area's profitable orchards. It's perfect for a picnic as well as sailing and windsurfing.

EAST OF PORTIMÃO

Lagoa, a sizeable town east of Portimão, is the province's wine capital. The acidic *vinhos da casa* served in most restaurants

The busy beach at Carvoeiro

on the Algarve come from here. Lagoa wine, both red and white, is more powerful than ordinary wine, and the extra degree or two of alcoholic content can creep up on you. The local cooperative (Unica Adega de Cooperativa do Algarve; tel: 282-342 181; Mon–Sat 9am–1pm, 2–6pm) offers tours of the wineries and tastings, with 48 hours' notice.

From Lagoa, turn south for about 5km (3 miles) to reach the charming resort of **Carvoeiro**, an archetypal small Barlavento resort. The small beach gets extremely busy in the summer months. A single road runs down through a pretty valley until it comes to a small crescent of sand shared by sunbathers and fishing boats. Above, rows of bright white houses perch on red sandstone cliffs, while cafés and restaurants fill the spaces in between. Carvoeiro is now fairly commercialised, but to many it remains one of the coast's most attractive resorts.

A narrow road follows the cliffs eastwards to the geological curiosity of **Algar Seco** ('dry gully'). Among other weird and wonderful shapes, wind and wave erosion have created a double-decker stone arch. There are walkways down to a lagoon enclosed by menacing rocks, and if weather conditions are calm, this open-air grotto is a paradise for snorkellers.

Continue east and you will find three more cliff-backed beaches whose relative isolation has thus far protected them from development. They are (heading east) **Vale de Centianes**, **Praia do Carvalho** and **Praia de Benagil**. The last one in particular is superb, and is approached down a vertiginous road flanked by massive cliffs.

Back inland, just off the main road, is the attractive little village of **Porches** ⑩, with some classic, white Algarvian houses and filigreed chimneys. Porches is famous throughout Portugal for its vividly hand-painted pottery. The shops of greatest renown are along the N125 route. Olaria Algarve (www.porches pottery.com; Mon–Fri 9am–6pm, Sat 10am–2pm), better known as Porches Pottery, is the biggest and best of these, with highly original designs and unique colours. Inside you can usually see artisans painting pieces. There's also an attractive little café-restaurant, itself decorated (of course) with wonderful ceramics. A little further east is Casa Algarve, which sells pottery and handicrafts in an attractive old house. More than others, it specialises in large-scale *azulejo* panels.

One of the most photographed beaches along this stretch is **Nossa Senhora da Rocha** ⑪ (Our Lady of the Rock). The rock in question is a promontory, boldly jutting out into the sea, surmounted by a little white fishermen's church. On either side of the rock are two lovely half-moon coves, framed by cliffs.

The beach of **Armação de Pêra** ⑫ is one of the longest in the Algarve – a flat, golden stretch to the east, picturesque rock stacks and small coves to the west. The massive development at the east end of town, though, has pretty much run rough-shod over the natural beauty of the area, all but eclipsing the former fishing village. On the front, however, there is a pleasant esplanade and a small fortress, built in 1760 and home to a pretty chapel.

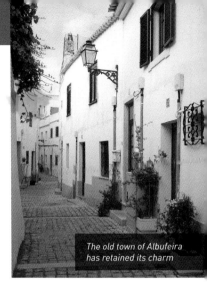

The old town of Albufeira has retained its charm

It's worth stopping in **Alcantarilha** ⓭, if only to look in on the **Capela de Ossos**, packed with a chilling array of skulls. For family fun, visit nearby **Aqualand** (www.aqualand.pt; daily from 13 June 10am–5pm, July–2 Sept 10am–6pm), a large water park, or **Zoomarine** (www.zoomarine.pt; daily 22 Mar–19 June and 3 Sept–1 Oct 10am–6pm, 20 June–2 Sept 10am–7.30pm, 4 Oct–4 Nov 10am–5pm, with exceptions) in Guia, offering spectacular shows with dolphins, seals, sea lions, tropical birds and birds of prey.

ALBUFEIRA AND CENTRAL ALGARVE

ALBUFEIRA

Once a picturesque fishermen's town, **Albufeira** ⓮ is nowadays Algarve's leading resort, full of neon signage and centre of cheap package tourism. The area now generally referred to as Albufeira encompasses the coast from beyond Galé in the west all the way to Praia da Falésia, just before a marginally distinct resort area begins at Vilamoura. Parts of the commercial sprawl, while rarely grotesque, still overwhelm the little town at their centre.

However, once you're off the traffic-squeezed main arteries, you will find that Albufeira's old town preserves some traditional charm: the cluster of whitewashed buildings includes a number of Moorish arches and three small churches.

Its magnificent setting – enormous, pockmarked sandstone cliffs rise above a huge beach lined with colourful fishing boats– has proved resistant to development ruin, though the sands host hundreds of sunbathers in the summer months. The gently sloping sands are perfect for family holidays, and if you are looking for a little more privacy you can escape the crowds by heading further east along the sandy coast. A tunnel links the centre of the town with the main beach.

The famous beachside fish market buckled under logistical problems years ago and moved just north of the centre. It is still worth a visit, however, and you will also find fruit, vegetables and flowers on sale.

Modern Albufeira has fallen prey to mass tourism – international bars, cafés and nightspots pump out loud music day and night, and there is little

Castle on the sea

Albufeira's name evokes the town's Moorish roots. Indeed, the North African occupiers called it Al-Buhera ('castle on the sea'). Its cliff-top position and labyrinthine street plan provided an easily defensible spot for the Moors, and Albufeira proved one of the last towns to fall during the Reconquest. Its layout, however, did not save it from the 1755 earthquake, during which the town was almost completely destroyed.

traditionally Portuguese about its raucous central square. However there are quiet spots to be found around town. And what brings all the tourists here, the beaches, lapped by the searing-blue Atlantic, are just a splash away. From almost any vantage point the view of old Albufeira sloping up a gentle hill and its seascape is incredibly spectacular.

Folk dancers in Loulé

With so much activity to the east, the excellent beaches west of town are relatively uncrowded. The best are **São Rafael**, a beautiful, sandy strip with some splendidly shaped rocky outcrops, and **Coelha**, **Castelo** and **Galé**, three small, beautiful coves.

HILL VILLAGES OF ALTE AND SALIR

One of the most picturesque settlements in the province is the lovely, flower-laden village of **Alte** ⑮, about 30km (18 miles) north of Albufeira. It is entered in romantic fashion, across a small, white bridge over a babbling stream that runs through town and waters a valley thick with oranges, pomegranates and figs.

The architectural highlight of the village is the 16th-century Igreja Matriz, entered through a classic Manueline portal. It contains elaborate chapels and rare 16th-century *azulejos* from Seville. The rest of Alte is the Algarve of postcards

Cork oak

Open any bottle of wine with a natural cork in it and the chances are the cork comes from Portugal. Over half the world's supply is produced here and you won't have to drive far in the Algarve to spot the cork oak. The tree is recognised by its broad, rounded head and glossy-green, holly-like leaves, or by the raw red trunk where the bark has been stripped off.

– white-washed houses along narrow streets, colourful windows, filigreed chimney pots and red-tiled roofs. And while their character may at first seem uniform, you won't see two houses the same. A small museum, **Pólo Museológico Cândido Guerreiro e Condes de Alte** (Mon–Fri 9am–5pm), pays homage to the town's counts, as well as its famous poet, Guerreiro.

Follow the stream upriver and you come to the popular Fonte Pequena (Little Fountain) springs, where a restaurant (www.fontepequena.com) and occasional folk dancing draw visitors. The setting is delightful and the perfect spot for a picnic.

If you continue east on the N124, you'll pass rolling hills and come to the pretty village of **Salir**, which is built on the edge of a steeply rising ridge and has two fine lookout points. The first is in the village itself, alongside the 16th-century parish church and water tower (don't miss the delightful gardens next door). The other, with the best views, is the adjacent peak, which once held a Moorish stronghold (follow signs to the *castelo*). All that remains of the castle are the bases of four huge turrets (12th–13th century) and some excavations. The old castle grounds are home to a tiny hamlet, complete with its own church. The panoramic views across to the main part of Salir and the surrounding countryside are spectacular.

EAST FROM ALBUFEIRA

Loosely grouped with Albufeira are beaches to the east. Here, the coastline features the last of the dramatic rock formations that have made the Algarve so famous. At appealing **Olhos d'Agua**, a single road leads between pine-covered cliffs down to a soft, sandy beach shared by a gaily painted fishing fleet, eroded sandstone formations and sunbathers. The resort derives its name from the 'eyes of water' that flow from strangely formed rocks, visible only at low tide.

Falésia is a beautiful beach framed by high cliffs, but to reach it you need to negotiate the grounds of the Pine Cliffs Hotel (www.pinecliffshotel.com), whose lift down to the beach is for guests only. There are other excellent beaches at **Santa Eulalia** (longer and more open than Olhos de Agua), **Balaia**,

The stunning Praia da Falésia, east of Albufeira

Praia da Oura and **São João**. The latter two are regarded as satellites of Albufeira and may well be where you are staying on a package holiday to Albufeira. The centre of activity along this beach hinterland is the infamous, brash and neon-lit 'strip' – a long street leading up to the hill-top area known as Montechoro. It's lined with a motley collection of bars, restaurants and nightspots.

Nearby **Vilamoura** is a wholly planned and sanitised community – Europe's largest 'from-scratch' private tourist undertaking. From high-rise hotels and sprawling villas that line manicured golf courses to the 19th-hole club bar and the Algarve's biggest marina, it is undeniably well done, but it could be anywhere. Still, it's a major draw for those who have their clubs ready for a golfing holiday; several of the Algarve's best courses have been sculpted out of the area.

As new as everything looks and feels, the marina designers were not the first to take advantage of Vilamoura's harbour. The Romans built a dock in the same place and established an important fishing centre here. The Roman remains of **Cerro da Vila** were unearthed across the road from the marina. Aside from some low-level excavations showing the elaborate waterpiping system and surviving mosaics and ceramics, there is also a small museum displaying everything from fishhooks to lamps, appealing to any student of archaeology.

A little further west, **Quarteira**, once a quiet fishing village, is today almost unrecognisable, subsumed under rows and rows of apartment buildings. The busy resort has a long, golden beach, and there are good, cheap restaurants in the old quarter where locals and visitors mingle. The municipal market still stands on the beach; every Wednesday one of the largest and busiest markets on the Algarve, offering fish and produce, is held next to it.

São Lourenço dos Matos

To the east of Vilamoura and Quarteira, the Algarvian terrain begins to change. The rugged, rocky lines of the Barlavento coast west of Faro give way to the long, flat beaches of the east.

The small crossroads town of **Almancil** has shops, cafés and businesses, many of which are dedicated to serving British expatriates. But the town, of modest interest itself, is best known for what lies in its vicinity. Many of these expats live a few kilometres south on the coast, and it is here that two of the Algarve's most luxurious and exclusive resorts are found.

Each is reached down long roads that become progressively more private-looking as the beach nears. **Vale do Lobo 16** means 'Valley of the Wolf', and is a security-conscious, maze-like villa community concealed behind a giant entrance gate. Guards do their best to keep the beach the domain of the expatriate and wealthy tourist classes. **Quinta do Lago**, a few kilo-metres down the coast, refers to the hotel of the same name,

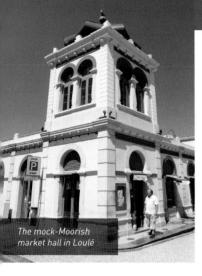

The mock-Moorish market hall in Loulé

once owned by Prince Faisal of Saudi Arabia, and the luxury homes that have sprouted up around it. Quinta do Lago has two of the finest golf courses on the Algarve and has regularly hosted the Portuguese Open. The beach is reached across a long, nostalgic wooden bridge that crosses wetlands and bird sanctuaries of the **Parc Natural da Ria Formosa**. On the beach is a terrific, if expensive, restaurant for fresh-caught fish, which you pick out and have grilled (www.julias-algarve.com).

SÃO LOURENÇO DOS MATOS

Back towards Almancil is one of the Algarve's top attractions – although if you're not looking closely, it's easy to miss. About 16km (10 miles) west of Faro, a simple white church stands out on a small hill overlooking the thundering highway. A sign simply says 'S. Lourenço', indicating the turn-off to **São Lourenço dos Matos** ⑰ (Church of St Lawrence of the Woods; tel: 289-395 451; Mon–Fri 10am–1.30pm, 2.30–5.30pm, Sat 10am–1.30pm, Sun 2.30–5.30pm). Inside is one of the most extraordinary displays of *azulejo* design you'll ever see. Every square centimetre of the baroque, 15th-century church – its walls, vaulted ceiling and cupola – is covered with hand-painted, blue-and-white ceramic tiles. Most date from the early 18th century and depict biblical scenes detailing the life of St Lawrence, born across the border in Huesca, Spain. The only element of the church not blue-and-white is the carved, gilded altar. The ensemble is a stunning sight, not to be missed.

LOULÉ

North of Almancil, **Loulé** ⓲ is a regional produce centre with a large Saturday market, known for its leather, lace and copper goods. Loulé is prosperous, with an ambitious, modern boulevard complete with outdoor cafés that are jam-packed on market day, and a popular summer world-music festival (www. festivalmed.pt). Coach parties come from far and wide to shop at the colourful, bustling market.

There are actually two markets. Fresh produce, including fish, is sold in a mock-Moorish hall, while a 'Gypsy market' is held towards the opposite end of the boulevard. Just below the permanent market halls, on the main Praça da República,

⊘ FILIGREED FLUES

Tourism has often been called an industry without chimneys, but not so in the Algarve, where smokestacks – graceful, lattice creations, reminiscent of Moorish lanterns – have become a trademark of the region. For hundreds of years, Algarve homeowners have taken great pride in the beauty and originality of their chimneys. The popular dictum is the more elaborate the chimney pot, the wealthier the owner. Originally carved of wood, later ceramic, and then eventually concrete was used. The area around Faro and Olhão in particular enjoy a strong reputation for rooftop art, but keep your eyes skyward and you'll see pretty chimney pots all over the Algarve.

you'll find a well-preserved section of the medieval castle walls. The ramparts afford excellent views from the town, and set into the castle remains is a modest local museum. Also worth visiting are the **Igreja Matriz** (São Clemente), a 13th-century Gothic church with 18th-century *azulejos* (tiles); the **Convento da Graça**, with a terrific Manueline portal; and **Ermida de Nossa Senhora da Conceição**, a small church prized for its baroque altar and ceramic tiles.

In the streets directly below the castle walls, you may well hear the sounds of craftsmen beating copper – which you can buy direct from them. You can also see artisans at work on the pottery wheel, producing leather goods and furniture. The craftsmen of Loulé are said to be the descendants of a community of Muslims who found refuge in the district at the end of the Christian Reconquest. If you are in the Algarve in springtime, don't miss the Loulé Carnival. The parades, 'Battle of Flowers' and musical celebrations are the best of their kind in the region.

The flower-lined road from Loulé to **São Brás de Alportel**, another market town and site of one of four *pousadas* (government-owned inn; www.pousadas.pt; temporarily closed) in Algarve, passes through rolling orchards of fig, olive and orange trees. It's best to visit the town on Saturday, when the lively market transforms its otherwise sleepy character. Try to fit in a visit to the lovely **Museu Regional do Algarve** (Ethnographic Museum), where exhibits of Algarvian costumes are well staged in a large, old mansion – built from the riches of the local cork industry – 90 metres (100yds) or so off the main square.

In this northern part of the province, life is visibly slower and more rustic; bonneted ladies in black walk along the roadside, old men ride donkeys, and families pluck almonds from the trees with long sticks.

The Palácio de Estói has been restored to its former glory

TOWARDS FARO

On the road towards Faro is a pair of historical sights. The **Palácio de Estói** is a charming rococo palace, which once belonged to the Dukes of Estói. Abandoned and dilapidated for many years, it has been completely renovated, and transformed into a new *pousada*. The salons have been retained as public areas and the São José chapel restored for religious ceremonies. Elegant grounds feature balustrade terraces and staircases with splendid bursts of bougainvillea, busts of historic characters impaled on the parapets, brightly coloured wall tiles and formal gardens.

The dusty **Villa Romana de Milreu** (Roman ruins of Milreu) is located 1.5km (1 mile) down the road from the village, on the route towards Faro (a small sign on the side of the road reads 'Ruinas de Milreu'). Some 1,400 years before the Palace of Estói was erected, Milreu was also the large country house of an eminent person. The knee-high walls that trace the outline of this once-luxurious establishment are still clearly visible. The tall, semi-circular tower ruin is thought to have been a temple to pagan water gods at one time; however, by the 5th century it had clearly been converted to a church.

FARO AND ENVIRONS

Faro ⓭, the provincial capital of the Algarve, is also the one that seems to get the least respect from tourists. Many fly into Faro, make a beeline for their resorts and return two weeks later, bypassing the city for the airport. Those who take the time – a day is sufficient – to explore Faro find an atmosphere quite distinct from the resort-heavy coast. Faro has a greater wealth of cultural and historic monuments than any other Algarvian town, a picturesque old quarter and best of all, tourists never overrun authentic Portuguese restaurants, cafés and bars.

Faro was always an important town, even during Roman times, when it was allowed to mint its own coins. It continued to thrive under the Arabs; its name may be derived from the name *Harune*, one of the old city's ruling families. The Christians recaptured Faro in 1249, completing the Reconquest, and the city prospered, becoming

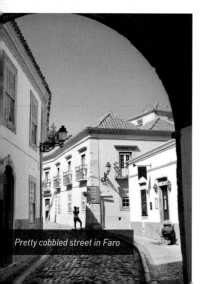
Pretty cobbled street in Faro

the episcopal see of the Bishop of the Algarve in 1577. But in 1596, when it was Spanish territory, an English fleet commanded by Queen Elizabeth I's favourite, the Earl of Essex, sacked and burned the capital.

Until comparatively recently, when the area silted into a tidal flat, Faro was a commercial and fishing port open to the Atlantic. Indeed, the Earl of Essex's fleet had sailed right up to

Arco de Vila and its stork residents

the city's Arab fortifications. Today, small fishing boats and pleasure craft must zigzag carefully amid the dunes and then creep beneath the railway bridge to enter the sleepy harbour.

OLD TOWN

The main entrance to the circular old town, near the harbour, is the 19th-century **Arco da Vila** Ⓐ, a lovely arch and bell tower habitually crowned by a venerable family of nesting storks. Beyond the arch, a cobbled street, worn slick by centuries of tramping feet, leads up to the splendid expanse of the **Largo da Sé** (Cathedral Square), best seen in the evening when floodlit and free of cars.

The only remains of the 13th-century Gothic **Sé** (Feb–Nov Mon–Fri 10am–6.30pm, Sat 9.30am–1pm, Dec–Jan Mon–Fri until 6pm, Sat 9.30am–1pm) are the unusual cathedral tower, main portico and two interior chapels. The entrance is at the side.

As you enter, look out for the remains of the Capela dos Ossos (Bone Chapel). Inside are some fine examples of *azulejos* and superb statues and carvings, one of the Algarve's top collections of 17th- and 18th-century religious art. Climb the tower for fine views over the whole of Faro.

Across the square is the **Paço Episcopal** ❸ (Bishop's Palace), an excellent example of the plain *chã* style prevalent during the 17th century. To its right is the *Câmara Municipal* (Town Hall).

The **Convento de Nossa Senhora da Assunção** (Convent of Our Lady of the Assumption) contains the most beautiful cloister in southern Portugal. The first Renaissance building in the Algarve, it was constructed in the 16th century on the site of the old Jewish quarter (Faro had a sizeable Jewish population in the Middle Ages). Abandoned as a convent in the 19th century and put to use as a cork factory, it has been beautifully restored as a museum devoted to art and archaeology, the **Museu Municipal** ❸ (tel: 289 870 829; June–Sept Tue–Fri 10am–7pm, Sat–Sun 11am–6pm, Oct–May Tue–Fri 10am–6pm, Sat–Sun 10.30am–5pm; free Sun until 3.30pm). The principal exhibit is a 2,000-year-old Roman floor mosaic measuring 9-metres (30ft) long and 3-metres (10ft) wide. Unearthed in Faro, it is nicknamed the 'Ocean Mosaic', for it depicts a bearded sea-god (though the bulldozer that discovered it in 1976 shaved off the lower half of his face). There are also busts taken from the Roman ruins at Milreu. Displays of Portuguese art are housed in the many rooms off the cloister.

Nearby is the **Ermida de Nossa Senhora do Repouso** (Hermitage of Our Lady of Rest), a tiny 18th-century chapel carved out of the ancient Moorish arches.

Just outside the old quarter is the **Igreja de São Francisco** (Church of St Francis), which was begun in the late 17th century. Narrative tiles adorn the main chapel and vaulted ceiling, which displays a terrific panel of the Coronation of the Virgin Mary.

The chilling interior of the Capela dos Ossos

TOWN CENTRE

In the centre of town, across from the harbour, the cobbled and shaded municipal **Jardim Manuel Bívar ⓓ**, created in the 15th century as Queen's Square, is a popular meeting place for young and old alike. In its centre are an open-air café and an old-fashioned bandstand. Several handsome 16th- to 18th-century mansions surround the square, including the Banco de Portugal building and the Palácio Belmarço (currently being renovated).

As in several other Algarve towns, the main shopping area of central Faro is pedestrian-only, and cafés and restaurants spill out onto the street, fish displays and all. Rua de Santo António is the main thoroughfare. At its far end is the **Museu Etnográfico Regional do Algarve ⓔ** (Ethnographic Museum; tel: 289 870 893; Mon–Fri 10am–6pm, Sat until 4.30pm), with displays of local handicrafts, reconstructions of rooms in a typical Algarvian house, and a colourful watercart that Manuel

Ignacio Miguel of Olhão operated for 60 years, almost up to his death in 1974. The museum sits on the edge of Faro's Mouraria, or old Moorish quarter. It's worth wandering the streets that lead to **Largo do Pé da Cruz ⑤** and the attractive little 17th-century chapel of the same name (Our Lady of the Foot of the Cross).

The new town, an expansion dating from the 19th century, is west of here. Two churches, which face each other across the large and congested Largo do Carmo, are worth seeing. The **Igreja de São Pedro ⑥** (Church of St Peter) is the smaller of the two, built in the 16th century. It has a carved baroque retable and a couple of rococo chapels.

But Faro's finest church is **Igreja do Carmo ⑦** (Carmelite Church; tel: 289-824 490; Mon–Fri 10am–6pm, until 5pm in winter, Sat 9am–1pm), which took most of the 18th century to build. The twin bell towers and stately façade are matched by a beautiful gilded interior, but the greatest attraction is the macabre **Capela dos Ossos** (Chapel of Bones). This 19th-century curiosity, like a similar chapel in the town of Évora further north, is constructed of the skulls and bones of monks, unearthed from the friars' cemetery. Depending on your tolerance for such things, it is either fascinating or sick beyond belief.

Less ghastly is the **Cemitério dos Judeus ⑧**, on the outskirts of town (off Rua Leão Penedo, near Praça dos Bomberos de Faro; closed Sat and Sun). Dating to the early 19th century, it has more than 100 tombstones in Hebrew, testimony to the once-important Jewish community in Faro.

Few people seem to do it, but it is well worth spending a night or two in Faro, especially if you've already spent some time in a traditional Algarvian beach resort. Watch the sun setting over the fishing boats in the lagoon while you have a drink in the splendidly old-fashioned, cavernous Café Cervejaria

Aliança, the city's oldest café. Faro also has some lively bars, catering mainly to the town's student population.

PRAIA DE FARO

Faro's beach, the **Praia de Faro**, is noted for its water sports. You can drive there across the single-lane causeway linking the long strip of dunes with the mainland (no buses or motor homes allowed), or in the summer catch a bus. If the sea is rough, simply cross to the opposite side of the sand spit and swim in the calm, warmer waters of the lagoon (though be aware, it can sometimes be muddy and a little unpleasant). Ferries head to Ilha da Barretta on Ilha Deserta (www.animaris.pt), an almost 10km (6-mile) strip of largely deserted sands off the mainland.

EASTERN ALGARVE

OLHÃO

Heading east from Faro, the first settlement of any size you will come to is the fishing town of **Olhão** ⓴ . A working port, it has made few concessions to tourism and is full of character.

Olhão has often been described as the 'little white Cubist town of the Algarve', its architecture likened to that of North African towns. That may have been the case some

Crumbling building façade, Olhão

years ago, but modern development has strongly interfered with its once-distinctive appearance. You can judge for yourself by ascending the bell tower of the parish church, **Nossa Senhora do Rosário**, which you'll find by winding your way through the narrow streets back to the Praça da Restauração (you may have to ask for access to the tower in the sacristy). Founded by King Dom Pedro II in 1698, the church has an impressive, scroll-decorated baroque façade, a brilliant white dome, stone bell tower and a chapel at the rear, **Nossa Senhora dos Aflitos** (Our Lady of the Afflicted), where women often pray when their fishermen husbands are away at sea.

Instead of the red-tiled roofs and filigreed chimneys seen elsewhere in the Algarve, the Olhão skyline comprises flat-topped roofs of terraces called *açoeitas*. Look carefully and you can still see the narrow, outside staircases leading to

⊘ AZULEJOS

It is thanks to the Moors that Portugal is so liberally endowed with glazed tiles, or *azulejos*. The name probably derives from the Arabic *Al Zulaicha*, or *Zuleija*, meaning ceramic mosaic. Other influences were painters from France, Italy and Germany, as well as Portugal's maritime empire.

Mass production began after the 1755 earthquake, but small family businesses using old methods continued, and still exist today. A fine example of the craft is in the church of São Lourenço in Almancil. Its interior walls and dome are entirely faced with blue-and-white tiles depicting scenes from the life of St Lawrence. Other examples are the tiled stairways in the gardens of the villa at Estói and the scenes from the life of St Francis in the Church of São Francisco in Faro.

white-washed towers, where fishermen's wives, or perhaps smugglers, would look out for the incoming fleet.

The name of the square, **Praça da Restauração** ('Restoration Square'), recalls Olhão's most glorious moment, when an improvised local army rebelled against Napoleon's occupying forces in 1808. This insurrectionary zeal subsequently spread throughout the rest of Portugal and resulted in Olhão being awarded the title 'Noble Town of the Restoration'.

Olhão's fishing port is worth a look. The fishermen of the town have a reputation for hardiness – some used to earn a living in the cod-stocked waters as far away as Newfoundland. During the past two centuries, however, some of the sailors have turned away from fishing and instead, taken to the cargo trade between Portugal and North Africa. This relatively recent link with the neighbouring continent may have been the inspiration for the local North African style of architecture. In any case, it developed long after the Moors had left the Algarve.

You're unlikely to see a boat coming in from another continent, but you are guaranteed the hustle, bustle, sights, smells and sounds of one at the **Olhão fish market**, one of the Algarve's best (the town is especially famous for its mussels and other shellfish). Adjacent to the market buildings are small, well-tended parks, one of which boasts several splendid benches decorated with blue-and-white *azulejos*. Just beyond the park on the other side, ferries depart regularly in summer for the barrier-island beaches of **Armona** and **Culatra** just offshore. These lovely, under-developed beaches are the jewels of the coastline between Faro and Tavira and draw large crowds in summer.

A little further along the coast, at **Fuzeta**, is another popular beach. The holiday homes here were destroyed in storms in 2010, but since then there has been reconstruction and rebuilding and the beach is even more splendid than before. Turn inland, because the small village of **Moncarapacho**, with a fine old church, a sleepy village square and a fascinating little museum, is well worth the 8km (5-mile) detour. The countryside around here is full of orange and almond groves and, as you head east (back on the main road) towards Tavira, olive groves and vineyards also

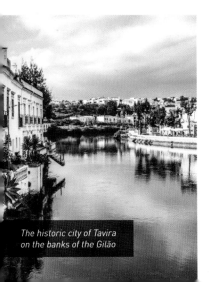

The historic city of Tavira on the banks of the Gilão

start to appear. Tavira's grapes produce a good, rustic wine consumed all over the Algarve.

TAVIRA

After the salty flavour of Olhão and the rural serenity of Moncarapacho, the aristocratic bearings of **Tavira** ㉑, one of the true gems of Algarve, may come as something of a surprise. One of the region's most historic cities, its Moorish, *Reconquista* and Renaissance roots are clearly visible.

In the 1500s, Tavira had the largest population on Algarve. This tuna-fishing port and self-assured town of historic churches, imposing classical-style mansions and riverfront gardens probably dates back as far as the Phoenicians or the Carthaginians. Its seven-arched stone bridge of Roman origin is still in use. Tavira's **castelo** (daily 9am–5pm, until 7pm in summer; free), in the middle of the *centro histórico* (old quarter), was a defensive structure built by the Moors. Climb the walls for a superb panoramic view of the city. Within the walls is an attractive, fragrant garden.

The walls look directly onto the **Igreja de Santa Maria do Castelo** (Church of St Mary of the Castle), most likely built on the site of the old mosque. The Gothic portal is the only original 13th-century part of the building to have survived the devastating 1755 earthquake. In the chancel is the large tomb of Dom Paio Peres Correia, who drove the Moors out of Tavira in 1242.

Across the square, the ochre-coloured former convent, **Convento da Graça**, has been converted into an elegant *pousada* (inn; see page 142).

Just down the hill, off Rua Galeria near the river, is the beautiful 16th-century **Igreja da Misericórdia** (Church of Mercy), a spectacular Renaissance edifice. The carved portico is especially fine, with a statue of Our Lady of Mercy under a canopy. The

Off to the beach at Ilha de Tavira

18th-century interior contains fine gilded woodwork and *azulejos*.

Rua da Liberdade, Tavira's main street, is lined with stately 16th-century mansions. A walk down any of the city's old streets will reveal handsome details of noble houses, such as double windows and latticed doors. A lively fruit and vegetable market is held by the banks of the River Gilão, and it is well worth crossing the Roman bridge to view more of the town's elegant houses and pretty flower-filled squares. Many of those houses have sloping triangular roofs, called *tesouros* (treasures).

AROUND TAVIRA

A nice excursion from Tavira is to the nearby island **Ilha de Tavira**, where there is a huge, lovely wide beach backed by sand dunes. Boats leave from Quatro Águas, 2km (1 mile) east of town.

Back on the mainland, a turn-off from the main road east of Tavira leads to a perfectly enchanting little whitewashed village overlooking the sea. Pretty **Cacela Velha** can't have more than 100 inhabitants. It has an 18th-century church, a telephone booth, a cemetery, an old well and a handful of well-tended, blue-and-white houses festooned with flowers.

East of here lies the resort of **Manta Rota**, a former fishing village, now full of new-build white-washed villas, pools and apartment blocks, and the high-rises and concrete of **Monte Gordo**. The reason behind all this development is a long sandy beach, which stretches undisturbed for some 10km (6 miles) between the two resorts and is backed by pine trees and dunes. Although the last in a long line of Algarve beach resorts (or the first, if you're coming from Spain) is not the coast's most attractive, the beach and water-sports facilities at Monte Gordo are enough to attract and entertain many serious sun-seekers. By night the casino is the focus of attention.

CASTRO MARIM

The Guadiana River, which runs into the Atlantic 3km (2 miles) east of Monte Gordo, served as a natural frontier for 2,000

⊘ ALGARVE'S BEST BEACHES

With the help of some insider advice, this is a round-up of a few of Algarve's finest sandy stretches:

Meia Praia A huge silver-sanded beach curving for miles, close to Lagos.

Ponta da Piedade A tiny bay surrounded by stunning seacliffs and rock formations.

Ilha da Barreta (Ilha da Deserta) Part of the beautiful Parque Natural da Ria Formosa, this deserted, wild beach is close to Faro.

Praia dos Castelejos Near Vila do Bispo, this breathtaking spot is known for its watersports.

Praia da Arrifana A glorious cliff-backed stretch, famous for its surfing.

Praia da Amoreira Another surfing favourite and a well-kept secret in western Algarve, close to Aljezur.

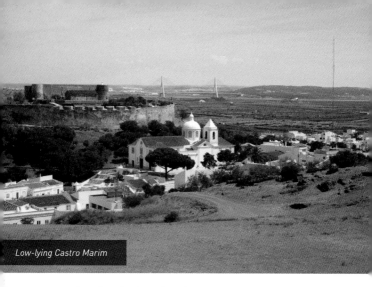

Low-lying Castro Marim

years, forming the boundary between the Roman provinces of Lusitania (Portugal) and Baetica (southern Spain). This explains the strategic importance of **Castro Marim** ㉒, a former fortress town rising from the flatlands to command the broad river. For five centuries its primitive castle-fortress was occupied by the Moors. After the Christian Reconquest it became the home of the new Military Order of Christ (succeeding the disbanded Knights Templars).

Below the castle, the saltpans and unpolluted marshlands of the local nature reserve attract a large number of waders (look out for storks, egrets and black-winged stilts). In 1991 a new suspension bridge across the river was built to link southern Portugal and southern Spain, and the formal border between the two countries has since been abolished.

It is worth driving north along the Guadiana for the pretty scenery and riverside villages. Alternatively you can take a boat along the river, starting at Vila Real de Santo António (www.rio sultravel.com). Timeless **Alcoutim** ㉓ is crowned by castle ruins and looks across at Sanlúcar in Spain, similarly dominated by ancient fortress remains. A ferry links the two villages and boats are available for river trips. It's now also possible to cross the border by zip-line (www.limitezero.com), literally flying over the Guadiana. Don't be caught out by the one-hour time difference.

In the remote hills to the southwest, the **Parque Miniero Cova dos Mouros** (2km/1 mile north of Vaqueiros; tel: 289 999 229; http://minacovamouros.sitepac.pt) is a reconstruction of an Iron Age mining settlement. The copper mines here were used for over 5,000 years and you can still see mine shafts, along with rebuilt huts, a fort and furnaces. Other attractions of this ecological park are the donkey rides, natural pools for swimming and marked footpaths for exploring the flora and fauna of the unspoilt countryside.

VILA REAL DE SANTO ANTÓNIO

Returning to the coast, the town of **Vila Real de Santo António** ㉔ (the Royal Town of St Anthony) is the last of the Algarve's beach towns before Spain. The city was designed to be as grand as its name suggests, in order to impress the Spanish on the other side of the river. The town plan

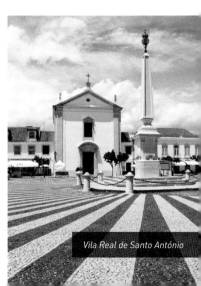

Vila Real de Santo António

was the inspiration of the Marquês of Pombal, King José I's favoured architect, and the town was built in just five months in 1774, aping the grid layout of Lisbon's Baixa (lower city).

The town square, the **Praça do Marquês do Pombal**, is the work of the royal architect and the tour de force of Vila Real. The pavement's black-and-white wedges of stone radiate from an obelisk in the centre of the square like rays from the sun. Distinguished three-storey, late 18th-century houses line the square, and orange trees soften the edges, adding colour and scent.

Today Vila Real is quiet but dignified. A walk around the old quarter reveals a number of fine, brightly painted houses along pedestrian-only streets. Vila Real de Santo António's main appeal is as the ferry port to **Ayamonte** across the water in Spain (www.infoayamonte.com). The trip takes just 20 minutes – less time than it would take to drive to over the bridge – and the white town of Ayamonte is a fine sight as you approach it from the river.

EXCURSION TO LISBON

Until the 19th century, the overland journey from the Algarve to **Lisbon** ㉕, Portugal's capital city, took a week or more. Now it's only two to three hours by road or rail, and you can fly from Faro in just 40 minutes.

Lisbon is a relatively quiet, easy-going capital. It's stunningly picturesque; there's plenty to see, great nightlife and some excellent restaurants, but it's all on an appealingly manageable scale.

The centre is small, compact and easy to get around in just a couple of days, and the town has two lovely old quarters that are as full of character as any place in Europe.

The city is built on hills – by legend seven, in fact many more – but the great thing for the visitor is the splendid vantage points

The lovely view from the Miradouro de Santa Luzia

and lookouts that these provide. The best place to start your tour of Lisbon is from the Moors' old castle, the **Castelo de São Jorge** Ⓐ, the king of all vantage points. From here you can look out over the whole of the city and along the broad Rio Tejo (River Tagus), spanned by one of the longest suspension bridges in Europe.

The castle is set just above Lisbon's most famous *bairro* (district), **Alfama** Ⓑ. Here you will discover a labyrinth of narrow, crooked streets, cobbled alleyways, decaying old houses, former palaces, fish stalls and bars totally unknown to the vast majority of tourists. Little has changed here in decades, if not centuries.

Another majestic view of the city is from the **Miradouro de Santa Luzia**, a park just down the hill from the castle. Nearby is the **Sé** Ⓒ (Cathedral), which has an ancient, cavernous interior – one of perhaps a dozen first-class churches in the city. Adjacent to the cathedral is the **Igreja de Santo António da Sé**, named for the patron saint of Lisbon, St Anthony of Padua.

Igreja de São Vicente de Fora

Just beyond the dense quarters of the Alfama is **São Vicente de Fora D** (St Vincent Beyond the Walls), an Italianate church and monastic cloister. The latter is the true highlight: its walls and courtyards are lined with blue-and-white *azulejos*, and the views from the roof are among the best in the city.

Down towards the river is the **Museu Nacional do Azulejo E** (National Tile Museum), devoted entirely to the art of painted and glazed ceramic tiles, a national art form. About 12,000 *azulejos* are on show here, from 15th-century polychrome designs to 20th-century Art Deco. A prized possession is the *Lisbon Panorama*, a 36-metre (118ft) long tile composition of Lisbon's riverside as it looked before the Great Earthquake of 1755.

The **Bairro Alto F** (upper city) is a hilly area full of evocative houses decorated with wrought-iron balconies usually occupied by birdcages and flowerpots. At night the district is loaded with an exciting atmosphere and is famous for its *fado* (folk music) clubs. It's a quiet, local-feeling area by day, dotted by cool boutiques and cafes, but comes alive by night as the city's major bar-hopping hub. The cobbled streets fill with people spilling out of the small bars, clutching drinks, and there's a party atmosphere.

Perched on the edge of the Bairro Alto is the **Convento do Carmo**, a convent devastated in the earthquake of 1755 but

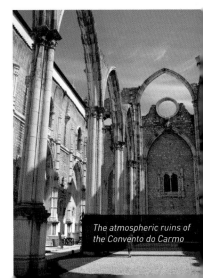

deliberately preserved as an atmospheric ruin and potent reminder of its impact. Nearby, the sumptuous, 16th-century **Igreja de São Roque** features a small museum of sacred art.

The convent used to be connected to the lower city by the landmark 30-metre (98ft) **Elevador de Santa Justa ⑥**, a lift situated off the Rossio square in the Baixa; however, the walkway linking the lift and the upper city was destroyed in a fire that swept through Lisbon in 1988, and nowadays you can only go to the top of the Elevador (definitely worth the effort for the excellent views). This 1902 Victorian marvel of iron and glass was built by Raul Mesnier, not, as popularly believed, by Gustave Eiffel. To reach the upmarket shopping area of **Chiado**, now totally rebuilt after the 1988 fire, you have to slowly meander up behind the Elevador.

The **Baixa** is Lisbon's principal business district. The main square is the **Praça Dom Pedro IV**, better known as **Rossio ⑪**. Look out for the railway station, **Estação do Rossio**, which looks like a Moorish palace with horseshoe arches, just west of the square. Two blocks north is another lively square, **Praça dos Restauradores**, which leads to the leafy main thoroughfare, Avenida da Liberdade.

The city plunges steeply downhill to the River Tagus

The atmospheric ruins of the Convento do Carmo

and its most imposing square, **Praça do Comércio ❶**, lined on three sides by gracious arcaded buildings and a vast triumphal arch. The grand square, wholly wiped out by the earthquake of 1755, has seen its share of watershed political events: King Carlos and his son were felled by assassins' bullets in the square in 1908 and one of the first uprisings of the Carnation Revolution of 1974 was staged here.

Moving west and down towards the river from Praça do Comércio is the elegant residential neighbourhood called Lapa. Its standout sight is the **Museu Nacional de Arte Antiga ❶** (National Museum of Ancient Art). Among its pieces of renown are *The Adoration of St Vincent,* a multi-panel work attributed to the 15th-century Portuguese master, Nuno Gonçalves; and *The Temptation of St Anthony*, a fantastic hallucination by Hieronymus Bosch, tempered with humour and executed with mad genius.

Some 6km (4 miles) west of Praça do Comércio is the riverside district of **Belém**. It was from here that the Age of Exploration (begun on Algarve) reached its zenith between 1497 and 1499, when Vasco da Gama's voyage to India opened up a major new sea route. During the following century, Portugal enjoyed a golden age of trade, and King Manuel celebrated the discoverers with two magnificent monuments.

The most famous is the diminutive but exquisitely formed **Torre de Belém**. By contrast the majestic **Mosteiro dos Jerónimos ❸** is Lisbon's largest religious monument and a formidable example of Manueline architecture. The church and its double-decker cloister survived the 1755 earthquake; in addition to housing royal tombs it holds the relics of national heroes Vasco da Gama and poet Luis de Camões. The monastery houses the **Museu de Arqueologia** (Archaeology Museum) and the **Museu da Marinha** (Naval Museum). Back down the street towards the town centre is the **Museu Nacional dos Coches** (National Coach Museum), housed in the former riding school of the Belém Royal Palace and a new modern building designed by Paulo Mendes da Rocha. The organic building behind is the **Museum of Art, Architecture and Technology** (MAAT). Exhibits are also displayed in the former Tejo Power Station.

Also in Belém is the modern **Padrão dos Descobrimentos**  (Monument to the Discoverers). This huge waterfront sculpture

Padrão dos Descobrimentos

depicts Prince Henry the Navigator at the prow of a stylised caravel that juts into the Tagus. The figures behind represent explorers, map-makers and astronomers whom Prince Henry mobilised to launch Portuguese ships into the history books.

Opposite the Padrão is the stylish **Centro Cultural de Belém**, which puts on temporary exhibitions and concerts. It also includes the **Museu Colecção Berardo** with a small but interesting collection of modern art. The restaurant here has fine views over the river and the Padráo dos Descobrimentos.

The riverfront **Parque das Nações** (Nations Park), designed for Expo '98, did much to reinvigorate the industrial eastern section of the city. The park continues to draw visitors with the second-largest oceanarium in Europe (**Oceanário de Lisboa**), an interactive science museum, a new casino and cable cars up to Torre de Vasco da Gama, the highest point in the city. The park is easily accessible by Metro.

The famous 16th hole at Vale do Lobo's Royal Golf Course

WHAT TO DO

SPORTS

The Algarve is a top destination for sports holidays. With great weather and superbly designed courses, the region has long been famous for golf. Tennis is also big, and some former big names in British tennis have taken advantage of the favourable climate to set up schools here. And with around 160km (100 miles) of south-facing beaches, there is plenty of scope for water-sports enthusiasts.

GOLF

Although a year-round sport on the Algarve, golf is played mainly from October to May. There are around 30 major golf courses (58 in total), many designed by the sport's biggest names. All boast luxury clubhouses, manicured greens and immaculate fairways. The top courses are to be found around Vilamoura and stretch west to Lagos. Green fees range from €45 to €200 (discounts possible) for 18 holes. All courses are open to visitors; most require an official handicap certificate and proper dress. For full details visit www.algarvegolf.net. Among the best courses are:

Le Meridien Penina (near Portimão): 36 holes. The longest and oldest course, with a distinguished championship history. Waterways and lakes dominate. Championship course, required handicap 28 men, 36 women. Tel: 282-420 200, www.penina.com.

Oceânico Laguna: 18 holes. Designed by Joseph Lee, opened in 1990. Known for its water hazards. Tel: 289-310 333, www.oceanicogolf.com.

Oceânico Millennium: 18 holes. Designed by Martin Hawtree to incorporated nine holes from the 27-hole Laguna course,

Golf packages

Algarve Golf can arrange discount green fees on a wide range of courses, as well as a variety of packages on Vilamoura courses, starting from €225. www.algarvegolf.net.

and opened in May 2000. Beautifully integrated into the environmental park at Vilamoura. Tel: 289-310 333, www.oceanicogolf.com.

Oceânico Old Course: 18 holes. Designed by Frank Pennink, this is a classic English-style course. Golfers must present a certificate of handicap no greater than 24 (men) or 28 (women). Tel: 289-310 333, www.oceanicogolf.com.

Oceânico Pinhal: 18 holes. Originally designed by Frank Pennink in 1976, and renovated by the American architect Robert Trent Jones in 1985. First 9 holes are among the pines, the last 9 have views of the sea. Tel: 289-310 333, www.oceanicogolf.com.

Oceânico Victoria: 18 holes. Opened in 2004, this 90-hectare, state-of-the-art course at Vilamoura is the longest golf course in Portugal. Designed by Arnold Palmer. Tel: 289-310 333, www.oceanicogolf.com.

Onyria Palmares (near Lagos): 18 holes. A challenging course with an ocean panorama, plus high hills and deep valleys. Views of Bay of Lagos. Tel: 282-790 500, www.onyriapalmares.com.

Parque da Floresta (Budens, near Salema): 18 holes. A spectacular rolling-hillside course offering excellent value. A favourite with families, offering a wide range of sporting facilities, a heated outdoor pool and a health and beauty spa. Tel: 282-690 054, http://parquedaflorestagolfclub.com/.

Quinta da Ria (near Castro Marim): 18 holes. Set in the eastern Algarve, with a stunning setting over the Ria Formosa, this comprises the Ria and Cima courses, both designed by Rocky Roquemore. Tel: 281-950 580, www.quintadaria.com.

Quinta do Lago: Two 18-hole courses, Quinta do Lago south and Quinta do Lago north. Among Europe's finest courses. American designed with outstanding lush greens and roomy fairways. Tel: 289-394 911, www.quintadolago.com.

Royal (Vale do Lobo): 18 holes. A rugged terrain with fine views. The 16th hole, with its cliff-top carry-over, is 'the most photographed hole in Europe'. Tel: 289-353 465, www.valedolobo.com/en/golf/royal-golf-course.

San Lorenzo (near Quinta do Lago): This 18-hole course was opened in 1988, and is considered one of the best courses in Europe. Required handicap, 28 men, 36 women. Tel: 289-396 522, www.sanlorenzogolfcourse.com.

Sheraton Pine Cliffs (Praia Falésia): 9 holes. Although not the most challenging of the Algarve's courses, it's certainly one of the most picturesque, with a clifftop layout overlooking the sea. Tel: 289-500 300, www.pinecliffs.com.

Enjoying the surf at Praia da Arrifana

Pestana Vila Sol: 18 holes. Considered to have among the best fairways in the Algarve, and one of a number of Pestana courses, which include Gramacho, Vale da Pinto and Silves. Tel: 282-340 900, www.pestana.com.

Keen golfers should consider the option of accommodation at a hotel affiliated with a golf course. Typically these are establishments very close to the top golf courses that offer free (or discounted) golf on courses on which it may otherwise be hard to get a game. They also arrange tournaments among their guests. Staying at a villa on the fringes of a fairway is another way to secure green-fee discounts and guarantee preferential tee times.

WATER SPORTS

Most of the larger beaches have equipment for hire, but don't count on expert tuition everywhere. Aside from the main beach resorts, there are good facilities at Praia da Luz (where the Ocean Club has its own water-sports centre; http://luzocean club.com), the marina at Vilamoura, Quinta do Lago, Praia da Martinhal and Sagres.

Jet-skiing. For more high-speed fun on the water you can rent a jet-ski at Praia da Rocha, Quarteira, Alvor or Quinta do Lago.

Sailing. Dinghies and instruction are available at Praia de Luz, Quinta do Lago and Portimão. Sailing is also possible on the dam, Barragem do Arade. For bigger craft try the marina at Vilamoura or the Carvoeiro Club. Anchorage and harbour facilities are available at Lagos, Faro, Olhão, Portimão, Sagres and Vila Real. Boat cruises are available in nearly all spots along the Algarve. **Bom Dia** offers Lagos–Sagres cruises, bar-becue cruises, dolphin safaris and grotto trips departing from the Lagos marina (tel: 282-087 587; www.bomdia-boattrips. com). **Algarve Cruzeiros** (Quay Q, Vilamoura Marina; tel: 289 301 900) run a variety of coastal motor and sailing cruises.

Scuba-diving. Reef, night, wreck, cave and freshwater dives from near Lagos are offered by **Blue Ocean Divers** in Porto de Mós. They also cater for complete beginners (tel: 964 665 667; www.blue-ocean-divers.de). You can also explore the coastline with just a good snorkel and mask. Other centres include **Open Waters Diving Centre** (www.openwaters-dive.

com) in Quarteira near Vilamoura and the **Divers' Cove** (http://divers-cove. com) at Carvoeiro.

Spa. Not exactly a water sport per se, but the spa waters at Termas de Monchique (Caldas de Monchique) have drawn visitors since the 19th century (www. monchiquetermas.com).

Surfing. The Atlantic rollers north of Cabo de São Vicente attract serious surfers; Sagres is more suitable for novices.

Angler at Praia da Marinha

Windsurfing. The most popular water sport along the Algarve coast; you'll find good instruction at Praia da Rocha, Ferragudo, Praia da Luz, Praia de Faro and Quinta do Lago. The last two have both open sea and sheltered water, providing the luxury of calm conditions.

OUTDOOR SPORTS AND ACTIVITIES

Fishing. The waters of the Algarve provide some of the best big-game fishing in Europe. Shark (mostly blue, but occasionally copper, hammerhead, mako or tiger), marlin, billfish, large bass and giant conger are regularly hauled in. Swordfish and tuna can be caught further out. Sagres, Portimão and Vilamoura are the main centres, where you can board a boat or hire a crew. One outfit to consider is the **Cruzeiros da Oura** in Qarteira (www.cruzeiros-da-oura.com).

If the deep sea doesn't appeal, you can rent a small boat,

rod and reel. The coast north of Sagres is one of the best spots to do this. You can also do as the locals do and use a rod and reel off the rocks at a harbour entrance or off the cliffs. Angling conditions are generally best from October to mid-January.

Football. The Portuguese are wild about *futebol*, as they call it, and the country hosted the European Football Championships in 2004 and won the Euro 2016. The biggest clubs are from the two major cities, Lisbon and Oporto. Two local teams, SC Farense and DC Louletano, play at Estádio de São Luís and the Estadio do Algarve respectively, both situated in Faro.

Horse riding. Whether you're looking for pony rides for children, treks for the competent or hacks for the inexperienced,

⊙ BULLFIGHTING

The main difference between the Portuguese and Spanish *corrida* is that in Portugal the bull leaves the ring bloodied but alive. Death does not come in the afternoon, but the following morning in the slaughterhouse. The Portuguese version is further sanitised in that the bull's horns are blunted to reduce the risk of injury by goring.

If you want the colour, spectacle and strategy of the bullfight but would prefer not to see the *coup de grâce*, then the Portuguese version may suit you. Be aware, though, that there is still a lot of blood, and the whole episode may well prove distasteful. The bull is used as a pincushion for long darts, then taunted and run to the ground. Bullfights have lost popularity in recent years and are held almost entirely for the benefit of curious tourists. The only resort which still hosts regular bullfights is Albufeira. The season lasts from May to September and the events take place every Saturday.

the mixed terrain of beaches, rolling hills and woods makes riding in the Algarve a delight. Most of the horses you'll encounter are at least part Lusitano, a sure-footed Portuguese breed. Recommended schools include **Albuteira Riding Centre** (The Stables, Vale Navio, 151H, Albufeira; tel: 961 269 526) and **Centro Hípico Vale de Ferro** (Mexilhoeira Grande between Lagos and Praia da Rocha;

Coast paths take in some lovely scenery

tel: 282-968 444; www.valedeferro.com). Also consider **Tiffany's Riding Centre**, Vale Grifo, Almadena (between Sagres and Lagos; tel: 282-697 395; www.teamtiffanys.com).

Tennis. The most prestigious complex is the academy at **Vale do Lobo** (tel: 289-353 000; http://valedolobo.com), which has 14 all-weather courts, including six that are floodlit. Close by is the well-equipped **Vilamoura Tennis Academy** (tel: 351-324 123; www.tietennis.com), which has 12 courts. The **Jim Stewart Tennis Academy** at Quinta do Lago (tel: 289-398 848; www.playtennisalgarve.com) has weekly coaching programmes on 10 hard and two synthetic grass courts. The **Carvoeiro Performance Tennis School** (tel: 282-357 847) on the outskirts of Carvoeiro has 14 courts as well as a pool and fitness centre.

Hotels with a good number of courts include the Alfa Mar, Praia da Falésia, near Olhos de Agua (15 courts); Hotel Alvor Praia, at Alvor beach (seven courts); and Hotel Montechoro, near

Albufeira (eight courts). Instruction in the pleasant surroundings of the Ocean Club at Luz (five courts) is demanding but rewarding. Portimão has seven municipal hard courts available to guests (tel: 282-418 780 for booking; www.tietennis.com/ctportimao).

Walking. The beaches and cliffs along the coast are excellent for walking, as are the mountains of the Serra do Monchique. Serious hikers might consider the **Via Algarviana** (The Algarve Way) – or at least a section of it. This challenging and often remote route runs from Alcoutim on the Spanish border to Cabo de São Vicente in the far west (243km/150 miles). For more information, maps and detailed descriptions go to www.viaalgarviana.org.

SHOPPING

Regional handicrafts range from copperware and cork to wickerwork and wine. The most famous items are *azulejos*.

WHAT TO BUY

Brass, bronze and copper. Candlesticks, pots and pans, old-fashioned kitchen scales, bowls and trays can be found. *Cataplanas* (bronze pressure-cookers used to make the national dish) make delightful decorative or functional souvenirs.

Ceramics, pottery and azulejos. Portugal is renowned for its colourful, hand-painted and glazed pottery and tiles, and such items are generally much less expensive in Portugal than at home. The roadside potteries on the N125 in Porches are the best source of ceramics in the Algarve. You can buy a single blue-and-white tile *(azulejo)*, an address plaque for your house, or a batch to assemble into a picture when you get home. Or purchase an entire set of plates. With several days' notice some shops will paint tiles to order if you have a particular design in mind or they can copy a photograph. But remember that ceramics can be heavy and fragile to carry home; enquire about shipping – some potteries will take care of it for you.

Cork. Portugal is the world's leading producer of cork. You'll find place mats, intricate sculptures and other designs – and it's all as light as a feather.

Embroidery. Embroidered tablecloths, napkins and other items are found throughout the Algarve, especially at street mar-

Colourful hand-painted pottery from the Algarve

kets, where they're likely to be literally thrust upon you. Haggling is absolutely acceptable at such places. Look also for the delicate hand needlework of the island of Madeira.

Knitwear. Despite the generally warm weather along the Algarve, thick sweaters, caps and gloves, most of which come from the north of Portugal, are some of the region's few genuine bargains. Stalls at the suitably windy venues of Fóia and Sagres are surprisingly good value.

Leather. There was a time when leather goods were amazingly cheap in Portugal, but prices have risen considerably along with the tourist influx and 'Europeanisation'. Still, it's possible to find chic, relatively inexpensive shoes and handbags. Portimão is known for its selection of shops.

Rugs. Attractive and excellently crafted hand-made rugs, mostly from the Alentejo region (north of the Algarve), are made as beautifully as they have been for centuries. The name to look for is Arraiolos, a type of colourful, rustic-looking wool rug named after a small town.

Wicker. Bags, mats, furniture, plant-holders, glass- and wine-holders, trays – you name it, you're likely to find it.

Wine. Portugal's wine industry produces not only excellent table wines from regions such as the Dão, Douro and Alentejo, but legendary port wine, which comes from the north. Vintages of port all the way back beyond your birth year can still be found in dusty bottles, but they are expensive.

WHERE TO SHOP

Many shops on the Algarve stock pottery and leather items among the usual trinkets and souvenirs, but the most interesting spots for genuine handicrafts or local goods are regional markets. These colourful affairs are a mix of everyday wares for local consumption, genuine local handicrafts, leather goods and clothing. Usually held once or twice a month in the larger regional centres, they are popular with locals and tourists alike.

Another option is to go directly to the artisans' workshops. These are becoming increasingly difficult to find, as when the old craftsmen retire, their descendants are turning to tourism instead of the traditional ways. Loulé and Monchique are probably your best bets.

Pottery and ceramics are found in and around every resort, but route N125 along the coast sells more ceramics and pottery than almost anywhere else in Portugal. The small town of Porches has a couple of the top shops in the country: **Porches Pottery** (tel: 282-352 858; www.porchespottery.com), which has revived and updated long-forgotten Moorish styles, and **Olaria Pequena** (tel: 282-381 213; www.olariapequena.com).

There are several large shopping malls, which continue to be a big hit with the Portuguese. The largest include **Algarve**

An evening out in Lagos

Shopping (www.algarveshopping.pt) at Guia, near Albufeira, Aqua Portimão, and **Forum Algarve** (www.forumalgarve.net) at Faro, both offering more than 100 shops, as well as restaurants, cinemas and crèches.

ENTERTAINMENT

While Spain's southern coast is a magnet for ostentatious jet-setters who party all night, sophisticated nightlife has never really sprouted in the Algarve. Most evening entertainment is either hotel-based or set up specifically for tourists in bars and discos. But in quieter spots off the beaten tourist track and in less commercialised towns, you're more likely to find locals out for a drink.

Popular resorts such as Albufeira and Praia da Rocha throb nightly to a disco beat, while visitors in smaller and newer resorts may have to rely on their hotel for an evening's entertainment. Lagos is one of the few resorts with a good selection of low-key bars and live-music venues. The 'Strip' in the modern section of Albufeira and the tourist village of Montechoro abound with all-night drinking and dancing opportunities – few of them classy – for sun-scorched tourists.

Casinos operate at Praia da Rocha, Vilamoura and Monte Gordo. They have restaurants with floor shows (open to families), while gambling takes place in a separate gaming room from mid-afternoon to well into the following morning. You must be 18 or over to gamble and will need your passport or identity card. Dress is not formal but should be reasonably smart. Games include roulette, blackjack, baccarat and the Portuguese game of 'French bank'.

Another favourite attraction is the *fado* night, at which distinctive Portuguese folk music is performed. You'll find them

⊙ FOLKLORE SHOWS

Folklore shows are regularly staged in the large resort hotels throughout the Algarve. Girls wear black felt hats over bright scarves, colourful blouses and aprons over skirts with hoops, and high-button shoes over white knitted stockings. The swift, whirling dances may also reveal traditional long underwear, worn in spite of the warm climate. Men are dressed more soberly, with trousers, waistcoats, cummerbunds and felt hats, mostly in black. Singers are accompanied by accordions, mouth organs and triangles.

There are basically two kinds of dances: the *corridinho*, or jig, which are whirling dances with stamping feet, and the *bailes de roda*, which are reels or square dances. Look in local magazines or enquire at tourist offices for details of folklore events.

at bars and hotels. The quality of performances is unlikely to rival the clubs in Lisbon's atmospheric *bairros*, but you can still get a taste for this quintessentially Portuguese musical expression. There are two kinds of *fado*. First, the melancholic, nostalgia-tinged variety, whose origins are unclear, which may have developed as a form of mourning for men lost at sea or may be a relic of the days of slavery – a kind of Iberian blues. The other *fado* is much more upbeat, and, while lacking the emotional power of the former, at least gives the audience a chance to wring out their handkerchiefs. Typically a *fado* troupe consists of a woman dressed in black accompanied by a couple of men playing acoustic guitars.

Neon-lit casino advertisement, Vilamoura

CHILDREN'S ALGARVE

The beaches of the Algarve, with long, sandy, gently shelving beaches for small children, and small rocky coves ideal for older children to explore, are perfect for family holidays. Pay attention to the beach warning flags, however. Green means the sea is calm and a lifeguard is on duty; green plus a checkered flag means that the lifeguard is not on duty; yellow urges caution; while red means danger and warns bathers to stay ashore.

The Algarve's beaches are perfect for simple seaside fun

Water parks are the most popular choice for children away from the beach. There are several scattered across the Algarve; the best are **Slide & Splash** (N125 Vale de Deus, near Lagoa; tel: 282-340 800; www.slidesplash.com) and **Aqualand** (N125, near Alcantarilha; www.aqualand.pt). Both offer an all-day bus service from many points along the Algarve. At **Aquashow** (tel: 289-315 129; www.aquashowparkhotel.com), there are theme-park rides and water attractions.

Krazy World (along the Algoz-Messines road, north of Albufeira; tel: 282-574 134; www.krazyworld.com) has an animal farm, mini-zoo, tree-climbing and crazy golf. Other attractions include **Zoomarine** (N125 at Guia, near Albufeira; tel: 289-560 300; www.zoomarine.com), which combines performing dolphins and sea lions with fairground rides and swimming pools, and **Lagos Zoo** (between Barão de S. Toão and Bensafrim; www.zoolagos.com), with animals and exotic birds set in landscaped gardens.

For older children, sports such as tennis, horse riding, windsurfing and even golf may prove to be excellent diversions.

Several hotels in the Algarve are popular with families and well equipped for entertaining children. Most in the Pestana chain have comprehensive 'Kids Club' programmes (with outdoor games, treasure hunts, etc). Perhaps the best set up of all is the huge playground at the **Pine Cliffs Hotel** on Praia da Falésia.

CALENDAR OF EVENTS

Portugal has a lively rota of annual festivals, ranging from traditional to contemporary. Each town celebrates at least once a year on its saint's day, so check at the tourist information office when you arrive for forthcoming events (a monthly events leaflet and other publications with listings are available).

February Lisbon: Fado Festival at various sites in the city; Volta ao Algarve – cycling tour of Algarve.

February–March Loulé: *Carnaval* – parades and processions, spectacular flower-covered floats.

March–April Holy Week. Palm Sunday, Good Friday and Easter Day – services and processions; Faro: Rally de Portugal.

April Loulé: *Mãe Soberana* – Pilgrimage to Nossa Senhora da Piedade.

May Portimão: Algarve International Film Festival.

May–June Various locations: Algarve International Music Festival – free classical concerts by local and international musicians, plus other performing arts, in some of the region's oldest churches; Alte: May Day festivities – folk dancing and markets; Estói: *Festa da Pinha* (Pine Festival) – wine and beer, barbecued chicken, dancers, musicians; Salir: *Festa da Espiga* – procession followed by fireworks and folk dancing.

July Loulé: International Jazz Festival; Faro: *Senhora do Carmo* – festivities and fair.

August Olhão: Shellfish Festival; Castro Marim: *Senhora dos Mártires* – festivities and fair.

September Silves: Handicrafts Fair; Pinhal do Forte Novo, Quarteira: Sardine Festival; Albufeira: Fishermen's festivals; throughout Algarve: National Folklore Festival – folk music and dance.

October Throughout Algarve: religious and trade fairs, including *Feira de Outubro at Monchique* (famous for its market) and the *Feira de Santa Iria* at Faro, a lively traditional event lasting several days; various locations.

November Vilamoura: TAP Air Portugal Open Golf Championships.

December Igreja do Carmo, Tavira: Christmas choral concert.

EATING OUT

Most Algarve cooking is as unaffected as a fisherman's barbecue: grilled or fried fish, chicken and steaks. Which is not to say the Portuguese are not inventive: you'll sample combinations such as clams and pork, sole and bananas, or pork and figs.

You'll also find the spicy taste of Portugal's former colonies has crept into the national cuisine. Chicken *piri-piri* (made from Angolan peppers) is a hot and very popular dish in the Algarve. Curries occasionally appear on the menu, originating from the former colony of Goa (in southern India) or Africa.

But mostly, along the 160km (100-mile) coast, you'll enjoy an excellent range of fresh fish and seafood. These items are no longer cheap, as much is now being brought in from distant waters. The humble but noble Portuguese sardine is an exception, and with a hunk of local rustic bread and a bottle of house wine, you can still feast well on a small budget.

Taking cover

Nearly every restaurant in Portugal serves a *couvert* (literally, cover) – an assortment of appetisers, including bread and butter, that appear to be free but are usually not. Your bill will include a charge of anywhere from €2 to €8 for the items. Theoretically, if you don't touch them, you shouldn't be charged for them.

MEAL TIMES

Breakfast *(pequeno almoço)* is usually eaten any time up until about 10am. **Lunch** *(almoço)* is served from shortly after noon until 2.30pm, and **dinner** *(jantar)* runs from 7.30 to 10pm (or later in a *casa de fado*). Snacks between meals are usually taken at a *pastelaria* (pastry and cake shop), *salão de chá* (teashop), or what the Portuguese call a 'snack bar' – a stand-up counter selling sandwiches, savoury pastries and sweets.

Because lunch and dinner tend to be major events, you may prefer the kind of light breakfast the Portuguese eat: coffee, toast or rolls, butter and jam. Hotels usually provide large American-style buffets.

Freshly caught fish

STARTERS

As soon as you sit down you will be served a pre-starter snack that may consist of bread, butter and a combination of olives, sardine paste and cream cheese (this isn't complimentary and will be on your bill as a cover charge).

Hearty starters always include a choice of soups – some vegetable soups, thickened with potatoes, can be almost a meal in themselves. Fish soup is variable but *gaspacho*, the Portuguese version of the cold Andalusian tomato-based soup, is usually good.

Fans of smoked food have two treats in store. The first is smoked ham *(presunto fumado)* – the best coming from Chaves, the northernmost province of Portugal (although Monchique ham is also highly regarded). The second is smoked swordfish *(espadarte fumado)*, which is a quite similar to smoked salmon but has a grainier texture and is less sweet.

Cataplana – a regional dish

FISH AND SEAFOOD

Besides sardines, tuna is the top fish along the Algarve. It is usually served as a steak, with almonds, or in a thick stew (*estufado*). Prawns, crabs, lobsters and fresh fish are always their own best advertisement, and you will see them all over the Algarve either refrigerated in a window display or, in the case of large shellfish, counting their days in an aquarium waiting for your selection. Most shellfish and some fish are sold on a price-per-kilogram basis.

Lobster and fish priced on a weight basis are often brought to the table for a preview. Unless you happen to be on an expense account, this is the moment to ask the exact cost. Large shellfish can be very expensive, so make sure you get a proper answer to avoid problems when the bill arrives. There are two kinds of lobster: a *lavagante* (with large front claws) and the *lagostim* or *lagosta* (the spiny lobster or crayfish, without claws). Similarly, there are two kinds of crab: the *sapateira* is a big Atlantic type; the *santola* is a spider crab.

Look out for the following regional seafood dishes:

Açorda de marisco. A spicy, garlic-flavoured bread-and-seafood soup baked in a casserole, with raw eggs folded into the mixture at the table (also served as a starter).

Amêijoas à bulhão pato. Clams, fried or steamed with garlic and coriander.

Arroz de marisco. Seafood risotto.

Bife de Atum. A beefy fillet of tuna steak, marinated in wine or vinegar, salt, garlic and bay leaves, then cooked with onion and perhaps bacon.

Caldeirada de peixe. The Algarve version of the French bouillabaisse; a rich, filling mixed-fish stew including potatoes, onions, tomatoes, peppers, wine and spices.

Cataplana. The region's most individual dish, named after the copper pressure-cooker in which it is prepared. The dish varies, but it is basically a combination of seafood, which always

⊙ BACALHAU

Cod, or *bacalhau*, is pretty much the national dish of Portugal. The Portuguese have been drying and salting cod since their first sea voyages to Newfoundland in 1501. Strangely, even though fresh fish is available on their own doorstep, they still prefer to ship in this relatively expensive, preserved fish. Preserving gives it a fuller flavour (though this is not always apparent when it is casseroled with many other ingredients). There are hundreds of recipes for *bacalhau*, the most common on the Algarve being *à brás* – fried with onions and potatoes, then baked with a topping of beaten eggs.

Fresh meat at the Loulé market

includes clams *(amêijoas)*, plus salami-style sausage, ham, onion, garlic, paprika, chilli, parsley and white wine.

Choquinhos con tinta. Cuttlefish served in their own ink.

Espadarte. Swordfish, often a grilled fillet steak. On some menus it's listed as *peixe agulha*. Don't confuse it with *peixe espada*, a long thin fish, usually translated as 'scabbard fish'.

Salada de polvo. Octopus salad.

Sardinhas. The best-value fish dish you'll enjoy on the Algarve; plump, juicy, crisply grilled and served with boiled potatoes. Note that fresh sardines are only available from June to October, though at Portimão you will get them year-round.

MEAT AND POULTRY

Cabrito assado (no forno). Baked kid; not a common dish, but worth seeking out. *Cabrito estufado* is kid stewed with tomatoes and vegetables.

Carne de porco com amêijoas. An improbable but excellent combination of clams and roast pork, probably invented in the Alentejo, but adopted by the Algarve.

Favas à Algarvia. Pork and broad bean stew.

Feijoada. A hearty Brazilian dish consisting of dried beans and cabbage stewed with pork, sausage, bacon and whatever else of the pig is at hand (often the trotters).

Frango piri-piri. What you most need to know about a *piri-piri* preparation is that it's hot. Chicken *(frango)*, usually, is cooked or basted with tiny red chilli peppers from Angola (you'll see them strung as necklaces in the market).

Galinha cerejada. Roast chicken served with smoked meats and rice.

Leitão. Roast suckling pig, served hot or cold.

Bife/Steak à Portuquêsa. Steak fried with garlic, topped with ham and a fried egg, and served in a casserole dish surrounded by sautéed potatoes.

DESSERT

The Algarve, with a ready supply of almonds and figs, excels at sweet desserts. Both are employed in a variety of cakes and tarts, including *tarte de amêndoa*, almond tart. Other sweets worth try-ing are *arroz doce*, rice pudding topped with cinnamon; and *pudim flan*, crème caramel.

Portuguese cheese *(queijo)* is also an excellent dessert. The richest is *serra da estrela*, cured ewe's milk cheese from the country's highest mountains. It takes three hours to make each small cheese by hand and it is only available from December to April. Outside of this you'll have to make do with *tipo serra*, a harder, factory-made cheese. Other cheeses include *flamengo* (similar to Edam) and *saloio*, a creamy cottage cheese. Fresh fruit is also at its best along Portugal's sunny southern coast.

TABLE WINES

Portuguese wines, while not as well known as those from Spain and France, are uniformly good, and several regions produce truly excellent wines. You need only tell the waiter *tinto* (red) or *branco* (white) and you can't go wrong.

Grape vines flourish in the Algarve

Vinho verde (green wine), produced in northwest Portugal, is a young white wine, slightly fizzy, light and delightful. A lesser-known type is red wine from the same region, bearing the seemingly oxymoronic name *vinho verde tinto* (red green wine). Both of these wines should be served chilled, as should Portuguese rosé, which is also slightly bubbly and may be either sweet or very dry. *Vinhos maduros* are mature, or aged, wines.

Vinho espumante is Portuguese sparkling wine, packaged in a Champagne-shaped bottle. Most are sweet but you can also find some relatively dry versions.

Several of the best wine-producing regions have names whose use is controlled by law *(região demarcada)*. The Dão and Douro in the north of Portugal produce vigorous reds and flavoursome whites. Wines from the Alentejo are also highly regarded. Of the local wines, you are most likely to see the Lagoa label, packing more of a punch than average wine.

OTHER ALCOHOLIC DRINKS

The two most celebrated Portuguese wines, port and Madeira, are mostly known as dessert wines, but they may also be sipped as aperitifs. The before-dinner varieties are dry or extra dry white port, and the dry Madeiras, *Sercial* and *Verdelho*. These should be served slightly chilled. After dinner, sip one of the famous ruby or tawny ports (aged tawnys are especially good) or a Madeira dessert wine, such as *Boal* or *Malvasia* (Malmsey). Two local wines that make excellent aperitifs are *Algar Seco* and *Afonso III*. Reminiscent of sherry, both come from Lagoa and are served chilled.

Local after-dinner specialities include *aguardente de medronho,* a brandy distilled from the fruit of the arbutus tree. Blended with honey, it's called *medronheira de mel.* Equally powerful is *bagaço*, or *bagaceira*, a firewater made from grape residue in the same way as the French make *marc* and the Italians *grappa*.

COFFEE AND TEA

When they want a coffee, most Portuguese order a *bica,* which is a small espresso. If that's a little too small for you, order a *duplo*, a double. Take one *bica*, add water, and you have a *carioca*; a few drops of milk transforms it into a *garoto*.

A white coffee in a café is a *galão*, served in a tall glass. In a restaurant you would order a *café com leite*. Tea (*chá*) has been drunk in Portugal as long as it has been known to the Western world.

Local brew

Portuguese beers are good and refreshing. Light or dark, they are served chilled, bottled or from the tap. One of the best and most common is Sagres.

TO HELP YOU ORDER ...

Could we have a table? **Queremos uma mesa.**
Do you have a set-price menu? **Tem uma ementa turística?**
I'd like a/an/some ... **Queria ...**

beer **uma cerveja**
the bill **a conta**
bread **pão**
butter **manteiga**
dessert **sobremesa**
fish **peixe**
fruit **fruta**
ice cream **gelado**
meat **carne**
menu **a carta**
milk **leite**
mineral water **água**

mineral
napkin **guardanapo**
salad **salada**
salt **sal**
sandwich **sanduíche**
soup **sopa**
sugar **açúcar**
tea **chá**
vegetables **legumes**
wine **vinho**
wine list **carta de vinhos**

... AND READ THE MENU

alho garlic
ameijoas baby clams
arroz rice
assado roast
bacalhau codfish
besugo sea bream
dobrada tripe
dourada sea bass
feijões beans
frito fried
gambas prawns
lagosta spiny lobster
lenguado sole

lombo fillet
lulas squid
mariscos shellfish
mexilhões mussels
ostras oysters
ovo egg
pescada hake
pescadinha whiting
polvos baby octopus
queijo cheese
salmonete red mullet
truta trout
vitela veal

PLACES TO EAT

The prices indicated are for starter, main course and dessert, with half a bottle of house wine, per person; service and value-added tax of 13 per cent are included, as they generally are in the bill. (Note that some fish or shellfish dishes, charged by the kilo, will be more expensive than the averages.) Except where noted, all restaurants accept major credit cards. Prices normally include taxes and a service charge, but it is customary to leave an additional tip for good service. There is usually a cover charge, and you'll also be charged for the bread and cheese offered at the beginning of meals at many restaurants.

€€€€	over €60
€€€	€45–60
€€	€30–45
€	under €30

SAGRES

A Tasca €€–€€€ *Porto de Sagres, tel: 282-624 177.* Open daily for lunch and dinner. This typical Portuguese restaurant, set in what was once a warehouse, is one of the best in Sagres for fresh seafood. Choose to dine on the sun-scorched outdoor terrace that overlooks the harbour or in the dark stone interior. Both serve the same great sea bass, lobster and grilled squid kebabs. Gratinated Sagres oysters and monkfish 'Tasca' are specialities.

Vila Velha €€–€€€ *Rua Patrão Antonio Faustino, tel: 282-624 788.* Open Tue–Sun for dinner from 6.30pm. Just down the road from the *pousada*, this attractive rustic restaurant has an appealing terrace and serves large, tasty portions of traditional Portuguese dishes.

LAGOS

Adega de Marina € *Avenida dos Descobrimentos, 35, tel: 282-764 284.* Open daily for lunch and dinner. Huge rustic dining hall near the marina, packed with locals who come for the lively atmosphere and excellent value charcoal-grilled fish and meat.

Dom Sebastião €€€ *Rua 25 de Abril 20–22, tel: 282-780 480;* www. restaurantedonsebastiao.com. Open daily for lunch and dinner (closed Sun in winter). On Lagos's main pedestrian thoroughfare, this very popular, rustic-style restaurant with dark beams focuses on seafood. It also has outdoor tables on the buzzy white-and-black-paved street.

MONCHIQUE-FÓIA

Abrigo da Montanha €€–€€€ *Estrada da Fóia, tel: 282-912 131;* http:// abrigodamontanha.com. Open daily for lunch and dinner. One of several good road-side restaurants with terraces enjoying panoramic views. Try the *frango piri-piri* (spicy chicken), which comes in mountainous portions to echo the view; or the *cataplana*.

PORTIMÃO AND ENVIRONS

A Lanterna €€ *Rua Foz do Arade, Porchal, tel: 963 229 161.* Open Mon– Sat for dinner. On the Ferragudo side of the Portimão Bridge, this long-established restaurant has a reputation for high quality, with elegant dining in small, traditionally furnished rooms. Specials include smoked fish and some interesting desserts.

Dona Barca €–€€ *Largo da Barca 22, tel: 282-484 189.* Open daily for lunch and dinner. This fish restaurant has an excellent reputation for delicious seafood and typical Algarvian cuisine – it has even represented the region at various national gastronomic festivals. The dining room is pleasant, with stone walls and draped fishing nets.

Julio's €€€ *Vale do Milho, Carvoeiro, tel: 282-358 368;* www.julios-restaurant.com. Open daily for dinner only. This upmarket restaurant has a sunny terrace and specialises in old-school sophisticated cuisine, with specialities such as fillet of fish *à l'archiduc* (served with shrimps and mushrooms in a cream and lemon sauce).

O Charneco € *Rua Dom Sancho II, Estômbar, tel: 282-431 113.* Closed Sun. No menu here, just large platters of good-value, excellent meat and fish dishes in a friendly, rustic setting. Fixed-price meals. No credit cards.

Praia Da Rocha

Churrasqueira da Rocha €€€ *Avenida Tomás Cabreira, tel: 282-484 005.* Open daily for lunch and dinner. *Churrasqueira* means grill, and you can get lots of grilled meats – including the famous *espetadas*, or kebabs – and the house speciality, chicken *piri-piri*, at this large place with good views of the beach.

La Dolce Vita € *Avenida Tomás Cabreira (opposite the Hotel Algarve Casino), tel: 282-419 444; www.pizzerialadolcevita.pt.* Open daily for lunch and dinner. The Italians who run this pizzeria claim it's the best in the Algarve. Thirty different pizzas to choose from, along with home-made pasta and freshly prepared salads.

Safari €–€€ *Rua António Feu, tel: 282-423 540.* Daily lunch and dinner. This popular sea-view restaurant combines good Portuguese cuisine with a distinctive Angolan flavour.

Praia De Três Irmãos/Alvor

Caniço €€–€€€ *Aldeamento Turístico de Prainha, Praia de Três Irmãos, tel: 282-458 503; www.prainha.net.* Open Apr–Oct lunch and dinner. Caniço enjoys a splendid location half-hidden among rocks, with spectacular views over a small cove and lovely beach. Staples include fresh grilled fish and seafood.

Restaurante Ababuja €€–€€€ *Rua da Ribeira, tel: 282-458 979; www. ababuja.com.* Open daily for lunch and dinner. Situated on the waterfront, near the fish market, this family-run restaurant has simple décor and friendly service. Not surprisingly, it's well known for its fresh fish and seafood but does unusual specialities including stuffed squid and cuttlefish with beans. The catch of the day is always a good bet.

ALBUFEIRA

A Ruina €€–€€€ *Cais Herculano, tel: 289-512 094;* http://restaurante-ruina.com. Open Mon–Fri for lunch and dinner, Sat–Sun dinner only. A 19th-century, four-storey mansion, 'the Ruin' features a basic dining room downstairs, rustic-looking restaurant on the second floor and roof-top dining with views over Praia dos Pescadores. Near the fish market, the speciality is well-prepared seafood. Try the *caldeirada* (fish stew).

La Cigale €€€ *Praia de Olhos d'Água, tel: 289-501 637;* www.restaurante lacigale.net. Open daily for lunch and dinner. Excellent seafood in a rustic, whitewashed beachside restaurant with an attractive terrace. Perfect for lazy and informal eating by day, La Cigale is elegant and romantic by night. Try the *mollusc a la cigale*, a shellfish special.

Paulu's Pizzeria € *Edificio Oura Cláudios, Estrada da Santa Eulália, Albufeira, tel: 289-587 159.* Open daily noon–11pm. A good place for a family meal out with good pizzas, pastas and children's menus. Alfresco and conservatory dining. Take-away available.

Restaurante do Hotel Vila Joya €€€€ *in Hotel Vila Joya, Praia de Galé, tel: 289-591 795.* Open daily for lunch and dinner; closed mid-Nov–early Mar. The restaurant of the most luxurious and sumptuously designed small hotel along the Algarve is, like the hotel, refined and elegant – and the only one in Portugal with two Michelin stars. To suit its multinational patrons, the kitchen prepares eclectic international dishes. Reservations for non-guests essential. Dress code casual elegant.

GUIA

O Teodósio € *Estrada Algoz, Guia, tel: 289-561 318;* http://teodosioreidos frangos.pt. Open daily for lunch and dinner. Guia is renowned for its chicken *piri-piri* dishes and this hugely popular restaurant bills itself as 'Rei dos Frangos' (King of Chickens). Be prepared for queues and crowded, communal tables.

AROUND ALMANCIL

Casa Velha €€€€ *Quinta do Lago, Almancil, tel: 289-394 983;* www.quinta dolago.com. Open Tue–Sat for dinner. The elegant resort that's grown up around it has only recently caught up to the chic standards set by this restaurant for nearly three decades. In a renovated 19th-century farmhouse (hence the name, 'old house'), this is rustic yet elegant, with tables outside on a pretty courtyard. The French menu is sophisticated, the dishes artfully prepared and the service perfect, but it's not at all stuffy. Excellent wine cellar.

Gigi Beach €€€ *Quinta do Lago, mobile: 964-045 178;* www.quintadolago. com. Open Mar–Nov daily for lunch. The setting is simple: a wooden beach shack tucked in among the dunes and wetlands of the Ria Formosa Nature Preserve, reached across a long wooden bridge. The food is also simple: point to the fish of your choice and watch it taken directly to the grill.

Pequeno Mundo €€€ *Pereiras (Almancil, just off Estrada de Quarteira), tel: 289-399 866;* www.restaurantepequenomundo.com. Open Mon–Sat for dinner. A beautiful old villa is the setting for gourmet French cuisine. Two terraces for alfresco dining. Favourites are the fish stew and the Chateaubriand.

VILAMOURA

Restaurante O Cesteiro €€€ *Estrada de Falésia-Vilamoura, tel: 289-312 961.* Open Tue–Sun for lunch and dinner. This terrace restaurant overlooks the glittering Vilamoura marina, so you can ponder the yachts as you sample charcoal-grilled fish and seafood items.

FARO

Adega Nova € *Rua Francisco Barreto, 24, tel: 289-813 413;* www.restaurante adeganova.com. Open daily for lunch and dinner. Hearty traditional Portuguese fare served at communal tables with jugs of wine. Great value and bustling, friendly atmosphere.

Tasca do Ricky €€ *Rua do Forno, tel: 919-117 057*. Open Mon–Sat for lunch and dinner. This small and simple restaurant (in fact little more than a hole in the wall) serves unusual and authentic Algarvian fare. Excellent fish and seafood dishes come in fair portions. Don't be put off by its surroundings, which are a little run down.

Dois Irmãos €€-€€€ *Praça Ferreira de Almeida 15, tel: 289-823 337*. The Two Brothers restaurant has been a Faro seafood legend since as long ago as 1925. This simple bistro has an extensive fish menu, including nine types of *cataplana*, and lots of regional specials.

Faz Gustos €€-€€€ *Rua do Castelo 13, tel: 289 878 422*; http://fazgostos. com. Mon-Fri lunch and dinner, Sat dinner only. Located in an old wine cellar, this gourmet restaurant specialises in local cuisine. Look for the good-value set and lunch menus.

Genibre e Canela € *Traversa da Mota, tel: 289-882 424*; http://gengibre canela.blogspot.com. This lunchtime-only vegetarian restaurant makes for a refreshing change, serving up delicious gourmet vegan and veg-etarian dishes. It's very popular with local people for its delightful buffet and Zen atmosphere.

TAVIRA

Bistro o Porto €€ *Largo Dr Jose Pires Padinha 180, tel: 281-402 955*. Open Wed–Sun for dinner. This is a charming riverside eatery that combines Portuguese and French flavours. Excellent vegetarian dishes.

Quatro Águas €€–€€€ *Sítio das Quatro Aguas, tel: 281-381 271*. Open for lunch and dinner; closed Mon. This handsome 18th-century building on the harbour is a fine choice for a seafood meal. Traditional Portuguese dining, with an emphasis on dishes such as *arroz de marisco* (seafood rice), *cataplana* and *octopus chowder*.

A–Z TRAVEL TIPS

A SUMMARY OF PRACTICAL INFORMATION

A

ACCOMMODATION (see also Camping, Youth hostels and Recommended hotels)

Besides hotels, which range in an official category from 1 to 5 stars (not directly related to price), you'll find *aparthotels* (one or two bedroom with kitchenette, occasionally called *aldeamentos*) as well as a selection of accommodation variously categorised by overlapping and confusing names. A small, basic guest house is labelled a *pensão* or *residencial* (pension); *quinta* and *estalagem* refer to an inn or rural estate, and *albergaria* is generally a 4–5 star inn. A *pousada* is a government-owned (but now privately managed) hotel, often but not always in an historic building. There are three in the Algarve – in Sagres, Tavira and the Palace of Estói.

> I'd like a single/double room. **Queria um quarto simples/ duplo**.
> with bath/shower **com banho/chuveiro**
> What's the rate per night? **Qual é o preço por noite?**

AIRPORT

Faro International Airport (www.ana.pt), serving the Algarve, is 7km (4 miles) from Faro, the regional capital. It's just a 10-minute taxi ride to Faro, and about half an hour by car to Albufeira. Buses (lines 14 and 16) leave regularly for Faro's Eva bus terminal, departure point for buses serving destinations throughout the Algarve. Taxi or minibus transfers from the airport can be booked at reasonable rates via http://polotur. com/ (sample cost for 1–4 passengers to Albufeira, one way, €30). You can pay online or on arrival at the airport. Airport facilities include car-hire agencies, a tourist office, bank, ATM and shops.

Airport Information, tel: 289-800 800.

TAP Air Portugal reservations, tel: 707-205 700; www.flytap.com.

> Where can I get a taxi? **Onde posso encontrar um taxi?**
> Please take these bags. **Leve-me a baggagem, por favor.**

B

BICYCLE HIRE

Most resort hotels have bicycles for hire. If yours does not, the major resorts all have scooter and bike rental shops. Among those are Formosamar in Tavira and Faro (Avenida da República, Stand 1, Faro; mobile: 918 720 002; www.formosamar.com) and Motoride in Lagos (Rua José Afonso, 23; tel: 282-761 720). Expect to pay around €20 per day.

BUDGETING FOR YOUR TRIP

The season when you go will have much to do with the cost of your trip. Hotel rates often double or treble during the summer months.

Accommodation. Hotels at the top levels are comparable to large European cities. In high season, a double room with bath per night in a 3-star hotel averages €100–140; 4-star hotel, €150–250; 5-star hotel, €300–500. Outside high season, many hotels are excellent value, and can cost half that much. *Pousadas* generally range from €200–400 for a double room (however, in low season a double room can cost as low as €80).

Meals. Even top-rated restaurants may be surprisingly affordable compared to most European cities. Portuguese wines are palatable and reasonably priced, even in fine restaurants. A three-course meal with wine in a middle-range establishment averages about €30–40 per person. Most hotels offer half- and full-board plans. Continental or full-buffet breakfast is nearly always included in the price of hotels.

Local transport. Buses and taxis are reasonably priced. Local buses are less than €2; a taxi from Faro airport to Faro centre (4km/2.5 miles) is €9–10 plus luggage (a supplement is levied between 9pm and 6am).

Taxis can be hired for day trips for set fees; check with the local tourist office for a list of trips.

Car hire. It's a good idea to hire a car in order to allow maximum flexibility, but be sure to budget for the cost of petrol, which is costly, as in most of Europe. Economy car hire is cheaper than in most parts of Europe; expect it to run between €20 and €50 per day (including collision insurance and taxes).

Organised excursions. These cost €20–30 for a half day, from €50 for a whole day, including lunch.

Activities. It costs about €45–200 for *golf* for an 18-hole championship course (or €50–90 for 9 holes); €55–60 per day for *big-game fishing* (spectators €40-60); *horse riding*, €30–40 per hour; and *tennis* €15–20 per hour per court. Instruction for most sports ranges from €25–40 per hour.

Nightlife and entertainment. Costs vary widely. Expect cover fees at clubs to range from €10–20, which usually includes first drink; casino entrance ranges from free to €10. Entrance to waterparks generally costs around €20–29 for adults and €15–20 for children.

C

CAMPING

Campsites are categorised from 1–4 stars. Public sites are open to all paying campers; private sites, marked with the letter 'P', are only open to members of the campsite operator, the Portuguese Camping Federation or holders of a Camping Carnet. Many of the sites are within easy reach of the beach. They range from very cheap, basic grounds to

Is there a campsite near here? **Há algum parque de campismo por aqui perto?**
May we camp here? **Podemos acampar aqui?**
We have a caravan (trailer). **Temos uma caravana.**

vast recreational centres with restaurants, pools and sports facilities.

Camping on beaches, or indeed anywhere outside recognised sites, is illegal. Details on all Algarve campsites are available from tourist information offices, or visit www.roteiro-campista.pt for information and prices.

CAR HIRE (see also Driving)

Cars can be picked up at the main airports where the major car-hire companies have their outlets. However it is normally cheaper to reserve a car in advance.

You must be at least 21 or 25 – depending on the company – and have held a valid national (or international) driving licence for at least one year. Rental companies will accept your home country national driver's licence. Third-party insurance is included in the basic charge but a collision damage waiver (CDW) and personal accident policy may be added. You will need to present a passport or ID, a recognised credit card or a significant cash deposit when booking.

A value-added tax (IVA) is added to the total charge, but will have been included if you have pre-paid the car hire before arrival. Third-party insurance is required and included, but full collision coverage is advisable as well. Many credit cards automatically include this if you use the card to pay for the car, but be sure to verify this before you leave home.

If you wish to drive in Spain too, you may need to pay extra insurance. A basic economy car is likely to average €20–50 per day (including collision insurance and taxes).

I'd like to hire a car **Queria alugar um carro**
for today/tomorrow **para hoje/amanhã**
for one day/a week **por um dia/uma semana**
Please include full insurance. **Que inclua um seguro contra todos os riscos, por favor.**

CLIMATE

The Algarve's climate is generally warm all year round. Winter evenings can be chilly, and July and August are fiercely hot. Spring and autumn are the best seasons to travel in the Algarve.

		J	F	M	A	M	J	J	A	S	O	N	D
Air	°C	12	12	14	15	18	21	23	24	22	18	15	13
	°F	54	54	57	59	64	69	73	75	72	64	59	55
Sea	°C	15	16	17	18	19	21	21	20	19	18	16	14
	°F	59	61	62	64	66	69	69	67	66	64	61	57

CLOTHING

Dress is casual in almost all parts of the Algarve. The exceptions are certain luxury hotels and restaurants, as well as casinos, where smart (though never formal) attire is appreciated.

Pack a sweater or jacket, even in summer, as evenings can turn quite cool. Winters are mild with the occasional shower, so a light rainproof jacket may come in handy. It's cooler in the mountains and also in Lisbon and its environs, so dress warmer if you plan on including these.

CRIME AND SAFETY (see also Emergencies and police)

As a major tourist area, the Algarve experiences more petty crime than other parts of Portugal, though crimes involving violence against tourists are very rare. Theft from hire cars is the most common crime targeting tourists.

Burglaries of holiday apartments, though less common than car theft, also occur, so be on your guard to the greatest extent possible.

As a rule, never leave anything in your car, even if it is out of sight and locked in the boot. Keep valuables in the hotel safe and refrain from carrying large sums of money or wearing expensive jewellery on the street. Do not leave bags and cameras unattended on the beach.

Report any theft to the hotel receptionist, the nearest police station, or the local tourist office. You must report any losses to the local police within 24 hours and obtain a copy of your statement for insurance purposes.

If you are going to Lisbon, beware that the city is infamous for its pickpockets, particularly on the Metro, the buses and Rossio square.

> I want to report a theft. **Quero participar um roubo.**

CUSTOMS AND ENTRY REQUIREMENTS

Americans, British, Canadians and many other nationalities need only a valid passport – no visa – to visit Portugal. EU nationals may enter with an identity card. The length of stay authorised for most tourists is 90 days.

The Portuguese–Spanish border scarcely serves as a frontier anymore and visitors can come and go easily, though you should carry identification. **Currency restrictions.** Under European Union regulations, travellers entering and leaving the EU must declare amounts of €10,000 or more. **Customs.** Free exchange of non-duty-free goods for personal use is permitted between Portugal and other EU countries. However, duty-free items are subject to restrictions: check before you go.

> I've nothing to declare. **Não tenho nada a declarar.**
> It's for my personal use. **É para uso pessoal.**

D

DRIVING (see also Car hire and Emergencies)

Driving can be the best way to see the Algarve, but, especially in high season, traffic can test one's patience. It can also be costly, as petrol and rental charges are likely to outpace the cost of public transport.

Road conditions. The southern Algarve coastline is served by the Nacional 125 (abbreviated to the 'N125'). Parallel to this road is the A22 or E01 (also called the Via do Infante, IP1), which runs from Spain as far west as Lagos. This road links in with the A2 motorway going north to Lisbon. The Via do Infante has helped divert traffic from the N125, which in summer can become a bumper-to-bumper nightmare. Exercise care at all times on this road; the accident rate is one of the highest in Europe.

If driving to Lisbon, allow at least three hours. In high season the motorway can be quite congested, and once you reach the centre of Lisbon traffic slows to a crawl.

Rules and regulations. The rules of the road are the same as in most Western European countries. At roundabouts the vehicle on the roundabout has priority unless road markings or lights indicate otherwise. Local driving standards can be erratic. Speed limits are 120kph (75mph) on motorways, 90kph (56mph) on main roads and 50kph (37mph) in urban areas. Cars towing caravans (trailers) are restricted to 50kph (31mph) in towns and 70kph (45mph) on the open road and motorways. Motorways have tolls (*portagems*) with one of two payment systems: Via Verde (www.viaverde. pt) or an electronic toll (www.portugaltolls.com). See websites for details.

Seat belts are mandatory, and children under 12 cannot sit in the front seat unless strapped into a special child restraint. You can be fined on the spot for not carrying your licence, passport, or car-rental documents; for ignoring parking restrictions; for using mobile phones without hands-free equipment; and for drink-driving (limit 0.5mg/l).

If you take your own car, you need only your national driving licence, car registration papers and an International Motor Insurance certificate. Comprehensive coverage is highly recommended. A warning triangle is also compulsory.

Fuel. Fuel by the litre is expensive in Portugal. Prices should be the same – or very close to it – everywhere you go. Some petrol stations are 24-hour, and all accept credit cards. Filling up anywhere near the N125 is easy, but petrol stations are sparse in some inland regions.

Parking. Parking in most towns and resorts is manageable. Don't disregard no-parking signs: your car may be towed away. Certain areas are metered and others are 'Blue Zones' where you must buy a ticket from a machine. Car parks and garages are also available.

If you need help. There are orange SOS telephones stationed about every 3km (2 miles) on main roads. If you belong to a motoring organisation affiliated with the Automóvel Clube de Portugal (tel: 707 509 510; www.acp.pt), you can make use of their services free of charge. The emergency number for police and ambulance is **112**.

Road signs. Standard international pictograms are used in Portugal, but you might also encounter the following signs:

alto halt

cruzamento crossroads

curva perigosa dangerous bend

desvio diversion

encruzilhada crossroads

estacionamento permitido parking allowed

estacionamento proíbido no parking

guiar com cuidado drive with care

obras/fim de obras road works (men working)/end of road works

paragem de autocarro sus stop

pare stop

passagem proíbida no entry

pedestres/peões pedestrians

perigo danger

posto de socorros first-aid post

proibida a entrada no entry

saída de camiões lorry (truck) exit

seguir pela direita/esquerda keep right/left

sem saída no through road

sentido proíbido no entry

sentido único one-way street

silêncio silence zone

stop stop

trabalhos road works (men working)
trânsito proíbido no through traffic
velocidade máxima maximum speed

Are we on the right road for ...? **É esta a estrada para ...?**
Fill the tank with super, please. **Encha o depósito de super, por favor.**
Check the oil/tyres/ battery, please. **Verifique o óleo/os pneus/a bateria, se faz favor.**
I've broken down. **O meu carro está avariado.**
There's been an accident. **Houve um acidente.**

E

ELECTRICITY

Standard throughout Portugal is 220-volt, 50-cycle AC. US and British appliances may require an adaptor, and those from North America will also need a transformer.

EMBASSIES AND CONSULATES

Consulates in the Algarve:
British Vice Consulate (Consulado da Grã Bretanha, which handles Commonwealth nationals): Apartado 609, Edificio A Fabrica, Avenida Guanaré, Portimão; tel: 282 490 750.
Canadian Consulate (Consulado de Canadá): Rua Frei Lourenço de Sta Maria 1, 1st floor, Portado 79; Faro; tel: 289-803 757).
Embassies in Lisbon:
Australia: Av. da Liberdade 200; tel: 213-101 500.
Canada (Embassy/Consulate): Av. da Liberdade 196–200, 2nd floor; tel: 213-164 600.
Republic of Ireland (Embassy/Consulate): Avenida da Liberdade, No.

200; tel: 213-308 200.

South Africa (Embassy): Avenida Luís Bivar 10/10 A; tel: 213-192 200.

United Kingdom (Embassy): Rua de São Bernardo 33; tel: 213-924 000.

USA (Embassy/Consulate): Avenida das Forças Armadas 16; tel: 217-273-300.

Most embassies and consulates are open Mon–Fri from 9 or 10am until 4.30 or 5pm, with a break in the middle of the day of 1–3 hours.

EMERGENCIES

Dial **112** for medical, police and general emergencies in the whole of Portugal.

The hospitals at Faro (tel: 289-891 100) and Portimão (tel: 707 282 828) have *bancos de urgência* (emergency wards). Some hospitals can also handle dental emergencies. For trouble on the road such as a breakdown, see page 119.

G

GAY AND LESBIAN TRAVELLERS

In a country heavily influenced by the Catholic Church, attitudes towards gays are not as tolerant as elsewhere in Europe, though in tourist-dominated enclaves of the Algarve, such as 'the Strip' in Albufeira, gay travellers will find accommodating bars and restaurants. The website www.portugalgay.pt contains a travel guide with information in English and other languages.

GETTING TO THE ALGARVE (see also Airport)

Air travel. Faro International Airport is served by numerous low cost, charter and scheduled airlines from the UK, operating from over 25 airports. TAP Portugal (www.flytap.com), the national Portuguese airline, operates daily flights from Heathrow to Faro; British Airways (www.ba.com) has a service at least once daily from Gatwick to Faro. Low-cost carriers include easyJet (www.easyjet.com), Monarch Airlines (www.monarch.

co.uk), Jet2.com (www.jet2.com), Ryanair (www.ryanair.com), Thomson Airways (www.thomson.co.uk) and Thomas Cook (www.flythomascook. com). From the US, direct flights to Portugal are from New York, Miami and Boston to Lisbon or Porto, with connecting flights to Faro.

Faro International Airport is 7km (4 miles) from Faro, the regional capital. For airport information, tel: 289-800 800.

By car. Many travellers each year take their cars from other points in Europe by major highways through Spain and Portugal. British travellers can take their car across the Channel to France or Belgium and make the drive from there, although the trip is likely to take 3 or 4 days.

The distance from Calais to the Algarve is over 2,000km (1,250 miles). You can cut driving time by taking the car-ferry service from Plymouth to Santander in northern Spain (a 20-hour trip), but this still leaves a drive of over 10 hours to the Algarve.

By rail. The Portuguese national railway network is called Comboios de Portugal (tel: 707 210 220; www.cp.pt). Portugal is linked to the European railway network; connections to Lisbon are possible from points throughout Spain, France and the rest of continental Europe. Travel to and within Portugal is included on any InterRail Pass.

London to Lisbon by rail takes around 24 hours, going via Eurostar to Paris, from Paris to Irún on the Spanish border by TGV and from Irún to Lisbon on the Sud-Express (for details see www.seat61.com). Lisbon and the Algarve are now linked by a direct, high-speed train. The service departs twice a day from Lisbon's Oriente station. The journey time to Albufeira/Faro is 2.5–3 hours.

By sea. Lisbon is a major port, and several cruise ships include a port-of-call in the capital. From Britain, Brittany Ferries (www.brittany-ferries.co.uk) sail weekly from Plymouth and Portsmouth to Santander in northern Spain (around 20 hours) The drive from Santander to the Algarve is likely to take another 10 to 18 hours.

GUIDES AND TOURS

A number of guided day-trip itineraries are available through almost all hotels and a myriad of local travel agencies and tour operators. These include: Seville in Spain, Lisbon, the River Guadiana, Silves and Monchique, Sagres, Lagos and the west, Loulé market and Alte, and jeep safaris. If you would like a personal guide to a particular place, the nearest tourist office should be able to direct you to qualified local guides, and often offer local guided walks. Day trips can be arranged with taxi drivers at set fees; again, see the local tourist information office for details.

Boat trips exploring the nooks and crannies of the famous Barlavento (west) coast are a popular choice; they depart from several points west of Vilamoura, most notably from Portimão.

> We'd like an English-speaking interpreter/an English interpreter. **Queremos um intérprete que fale inglês/ um intérprete inglês.**

H

HEALTH AND MEDICAL CARE (see also Emergencies)

Standards of hygiene are generally very high; the most likely illness to befall travellers will be due to an excess of sun or alcohol. Tap water is safe to drink, but bottled water is always safest and is available everywhere. Even most local people drink bottled water, either *água com gas* (carbonated) or *sem gas* (still).

Farmácias (chemists) are open during normal business hours and are recognisable by an illuminated green cross sign. At other times one shop in each neighbourhood is on duty round the clock. Addresses are listed in newspapers.

For more serious illness or injury, all principal Algarve towns and resorts have hospitals, and many doctors are multilingual (most can speak English remarkably well). There are also a number of expatriate doctors at medical clinics and health centres throughout the region. Tourist offices carry lists of English-speaking doctors. The Red Cross (*Cruz Vermelha*) can be contacted in Faro (tel: 289-899 903) and Portimão (tel: 282-485 640).

Medical insurance to cover illness or accident while abroad is a good investment. EU nationals with a European Health Insurance Card (EHIC) obtained before departure can receive free emergency treatment at Social Security and Municipal hospitals in Portugal.

Where's the nearest (all-night) pharmacy? **Onde fica a farmácia (de serviço) mais próxima?**
I need a doctor/dentist. **Preciso de um médico/uma dentista.**
I'm not feeling well. **Não me sinto bem.**
an ambulance **ambulância**
hospital **hospital**
an upset stomach **mal do estômago**
sunstroke **uma insolação**

HOLIDAYS

National holidays:
1 January *Ano Novo* New Year's Day
25 April *Dia da Liberdade* Revolution Day
1 May *Dia do Trabalho* Labour Day
10 June *Dia de Portugal* National Day
15 August *Assunção* Assumption
5 October *Heróis da República* Republic Day
1 November *Todos-os-Santos* All Saints' Day
1 December *Dia da Independência* Independence Day
8 December *Imaculada Conceição* Immaculate Conception
25 December *Natal* Christmas Day
Movable dates:
Carnaval Shrove Tuesday

Sexta-feira Santa Good Friday
Corpo de Deus Corpus Christi

In addition, every town closes down and takes to the streets at least once a year in honour of its own patron saint. See the Calendar of Events for other events, page 95.

> Are you open tomorrow? **Estão abertos amanhã?**
> When do you close? **Quando fecha?**

L

LANGUAGE

The Portuguese in Portugal is much more closed and guttural-sounding and is also spoken much faster than that in Brazil. A large number of people in the Algarve speak passable and even fluent English.

M

MAPS

The red, green and yellow 'Portugal Tourist Map', available at some tourist information offices, is a map of the entire country; you may need a magnifying glass for the smaller roads in the Algarve. Otherwise, to explore roads less travelled, the 'Turinta' map of the Algarve (1:176,000) is a good buy, and also consider the laminated Insight 'Fleximap' of the Algarve (1:215,000). All tourist information offices will supply you with a reasonable street plan of the local town.

> a street map of... **um mapa de...**
> a road map of the Algarve **um mapa das estradas do Algarve**

TRAVEL TIPS

MEDIA

Foreign newspapers usually arrive the day after publication, though European editions of the *Guardian* and *Financial Times* and the *International Herald Tribune* are available on the same day at many newsagents. Popular foreign magazines are also available. The most important Portuguese-language daily is *Diário de Notícias,* which contains full cultural listings.

English-language publications with useful information as to what's on (folklore, markets, music, cinema, sporting events, etc) include: *The Resident* (http://portugalresident.com), a weekly magazine; and the bi-monthly glossy *Essential Algarve.* The weekend *Portugal News* is the country's largest-circulation Englishlanguage newspaper, also available online at www.the-news.net.

There are two government-operated TV channels in Portugal. Most hotels and some bars also have cable connections showing world news, feature films, football games and other big sporting events.

MONEY (see also Budgeting for your trip)

Currency *(moeda).* The euro (€) is the official currency used in Portugal. Notes are denominated in 5, 10, 20, 50, 100 and 500 euros; coins in 1 and 2 euros and 1, 2, 5, 10, 20 and 50 cents *(cêntimos).*

Currency exchange *(banco; câmbio).* Normal banking hours are Monday–Friday 8.30am–3pm. Some banks remain open later and at weekends to change money. The exchange at Faro airport is open daily 6am– midnight. Changing money can be quite expensive, and you are advised to check the rate of commission before any transaction. Banks often levy 0.5 percent commission with a minimum charge of €10, so it is not a good idea to exchange small amounts with them. Automatic money-exchanging machines (ATMs) charge at least 2 percent commission.

Credit cards *(cartão de crédito).* Standard international credit cards are widely accepted, as are Eurocheque cards. However, in some shops and restaurants, especially in small villages, you may not be able to use a credit card.

ATMs *(caixa automática).* Automatic teller machines outside banks, identified by the MB (MultiBanco) sign, are widely available. You can get cash with a Visa or Mastercard, or another card on an international network like Cirrus, as long as your card has a four-digit PIN.

Travellers' cheques. Travellers' cheques are not widely accepted and a high flat-rate fee is charged for changing them. Paying by cheque is invariably more expensive than by cash, due to the lower rate of exchange. You will need to show your passport.

> Can I pay with this credit card? **Posso pagar com cartão de crédito?**
> I want to change some pounds/dollars. **Queria trocar libras/dólares.**
> Can you cash a traveller's cheque? **Pode pagar um cheque de viagem?**

O

OPENING HOURS

Most shops and offices open 9/10am–7pm on weekdays (some take a lunch break between 1 and 3pm) and 9am–1pm on Saturday. In summer many shops will remain open all day, and until 10pm or later. Shopping malls open from 10am–10pm or even midnight. Most museums open 10am–6pm (some might take a lunch break). Most public museums are closed on Monday or Tuesday. Churches normally open from 7am–noon and 4–7pm Monday to Saturday and are open for Mass on Sunday.

The Portuguese do not take a siesta, but most businesses close for a 1–2-hour lunch break. Banks are open 8.30am–3pm Monday– Friday. In resorts many bars are open from noon (or earlier) until the wee hours. Informal restaurants may open all day but more upscale establishments tend to only open at lunch and in the evening, or for dinner only. Some restaurants close one day a week, so check first.

P

POLICE (see also Emergencies)

Police wearing armbands marked cd (it stands for Corpo Distrital, meaning local corps) are assigned to assist tourists and normally speak at least a smidgen of a foreign language.

On highways, traffic is controlled by the Guarda Nacional Republicana (GNR) in white cars or on motorcycles. For a general emergency, dial 112.

Where's the nearest police station? **Onde fica o posto de policia mais próximo?**

POST OFFICES

The mail service is generally good, though it can get bogged down during the height of the season. Main offices open 8.30 or 9am to 6 or 6.30pm Monday–Friday; local branches open 9am to 12.30pm and 2 to 6pm Monday–Friday. The main post offices in Portimão and Faro open on Saturday mornings as well. For details visit www.ctt.pt.

Mail from Portugal may take up to a week to reach a European destination. There is also a faster 'Azul' service which takes 2–3 days.

Where's the nearest post office? **Onde fica a estação de correios mais próxima?**
A stamp for this letter/postcard, please. **Um selo para esta carta/este postal, por favor.**
express (special delivery) **expresso**
airmail **via aérea**
registered **registado**

PUBLIC TRANSPORT

Buses *(autocarro)*. EVA Transportes (www.eva-bus.com) operates most buses in the Algarve. Local and regional timetables may be consulted at any bus station or tourist information office. Most buses run on time. Buy your ticket on board the bus for all services except for the Algarve Express, where tickets must be purchased in advance at the station. Bus stops are denoted by the sign 'Paragem'.

Trains *(comboio)*. An Algarve railway line runs from Lagos in the west to the eastern frontier at Vila Real de Santo António, with 50 stations in between. Stations are in or near Faro, Portimão and Lagos, but in other spots are far enough away to require a bus or taxi ride. Intercity trains link Albuferia with Lisbon in 2 hours 30 minutes. For Faro add another 30 minutes. Fares are inexpensive: Lisbon–Faro return is from €44 (second class).

Train timetables are posted at all railway stations; request a *guía de horarios* for a full listing of timetables. Consult the website of Comboios de Portugal, the national railway network, for timetables and information on international and domestic trains: www.cp.pt.

Taxis *(táxi)*. Portuguese taxis are usually cream-coloured though some of the old black and green ones are still in use. While you can hail them

Where can I get a taxi? **Onde posso encontrar um táxi?**
What's the fare to...? **Quanto custa o percurso para...?**
Where is the nearest railway station/bus stop? **Onde é a estação ferroviária/a paragem de autocarros mais próxima?**
When's the next bus/train to...? **Quando parte o próximo autocarro/comboio para...?**
I want a ticket to... **Queria um bilhete para...**
single (one-way trip) **ida**
return (round-trip) **ida e volta**

in the street, it is usually easier to go to a taxi stand or telephone for one. The majority of taxis are metered. If your taxi does not have a meter, make sure you ask what the charge will be before setting out. Average taxi fares to all resorts from Faro are posted at the airport. Fares increase by 20 percent if you travel from 9pm to 6am and there are fixed charges for luggage carried in the boot.

R

RELIGION

The Portuguese are predominantly Roman Catholic, a fact reflected in surviving religious rituals and saints' days that are public holidays. Services in English are scheduled in principal tourist areas. Protestant (primarily Anglican) services are held in several towns. Full details of all services are available from tourist offices and most hotels. The weekly English-language publication, *The Resident*, has a full listing.

S

SMOKING

Smoking in public places was banned in Portugal in 2008.

T

TELEPHONE

Portugal's country code is 351. There are no local dialling codes; you need to dial all 9 digits from anywhere within the country.

Most public telephones accept pre-paid telephone cards or credit cards as well as coins. *Credifone* telephone cards can be purchased at post offices, newsagents or supermarkets. Local, national and international calls can also be made from hotels, but almost always with an exorbitant surcharge. You are wise to make these with an international calling card, if you must make them from your hotel room.

To make an international call, dial 00 for an international line (both Europe and overseas; eg. UK 0044, USA 001) + the country code + phone number (including the area code, without the initial '0', where there is one).

There is wide mobile-phone coverage in Portugal, including around the Algarve. The three major operators are MEO (www.meo.pt), NOS (www.nos.pt) and Vodafone (www.vodafone.pt). If your GSM phone is unlocked (which you can have done locally), you may choose to use a local pay-as-you-go SIM card for cheaper local calls.

reverse-charge call **paga pelo destinatário**
Can you get me this number in ...? **Pode ligar-me para este número em ...?**

TIME ZONES

Portugal, being at the western edge of Europe, maintains GMT (along with the UK) and is therefore 1 hour behind the rest of the EU. From the last Sunday in March until the last Sunday in October, the clocks are moved 1 hour ahead for summer time (GMT +1).

TIPPING

In restaurants where service is not included, leave a 10 percent tip. Hotel porters, per bag, generally receive €1. Give hairdressers, tour guides and taxi drivers around 10 percent.

TOILETS

Public toilets exist in some large towns, but almost every bar and restaurant has one available for public use. Large hotels are also an excellent place to find clean toilets. It's polite to buy a coffee or drink if you drop in to use the toilet but no one will shout at you if you don't. The Ladies' is marked *Senhoras* and the Gentlemen's *Homens*.

TOURIST INFORMATION

Information on the Algarve may be obtained from Portuguese National Tourist Offices:

United Kingdom: 11 Belgrave Square, London SW1X 8PP; UK brochure line, tel: 020-7201 6666.

USA: 590 Fifth Ave, 4th floor, New York, NY 10036; tel: +1-646 72 30200.

In the Algarve itself, all major (and some minor) towns have tourist information offices, staffed by helpful English-speaking assistants. The major Algarve regional office is in Faro (Av. 5 de Outubro, 18; tel: 289-800 400). Others include:

Albufeira: Rua 5 de Outubro; tel: 289-585 279

Faro: Rua da Misericórdia, 8/12; tel: 289-803 604

Lagos: Praça Gil Eanes; tel: 282-763 031

Portimão: Ed. TEMPO, Teatro Municipal, Largo 1 de Dezembro; tel: 282-402 487

Praia da Rocha: Av. Tomás Cabreira; tel: 282-419 132

Sagres: Rua Comandante Matoso-Vila do Bispo; tel: 282-624 873

TRAVELLERS WITH DISABILITIES

For information on local organisations and transport see http://algarve.angloinfo.com/information/healthcare/people-with-disabilities, and for information on accommodation, search 'Algarve' on the www.disabledholidaydirectory.co.uk.

W

WEBSITES AND INTERNET

Websites worth checking before you go include:

www.algarvemais.com; www.algarveuncovered.com General websites packed with useful information on the region.

www.cp.pt Comboios de Portugal, national railway network, with timetables and details of international and domestic trains.

www.flytap.com TAP/Air Portugal – the Portuguese national airline.
www.portugalgolf.pt; www.algarvegolf.net Sites on golf, with information specifically related to the Algarve.
www.portugalvirtual.pt General country information and tourism data-
base, with accommodation links.
www.pousadas.pt Inns of Portugal.
www.visitalgarve.pt Official website for the Algarve region.
www.visitportugal.com Official website for Portugal.
Internet. Most hotels, post offices (with Netpost system), conference
centres and shopping malls now offer hotspots with free wireless. Otherwise, ask for the address of an internet café at the nearest tourist
information office.

WEIGHTS AND MEASURES
The metric system is used in Portugal.

YOUTH HOSTELS
Four youth hostels operate year-round in the Algarve:
Alcoutim: tel: 281 546 004.
Faro: Rua de PSP – Edifício do IPJ, tel: 289 878 090.
Lagos: Rua de Lançarote de Freitas, 50, tel: 282 761 970.
Portimão: Rua Pousada de Juventude, tel: 282 491 804.

To book, or for additional information, contact the headquarters of
the Portuguese Youth Hostel Association (Associação Portuguesa de
Pousadas de Juventude), Rua Lúcio de Azevedo Nr 27, 1600-146 Lisbon;
tel: 707 233 233; www.pousadasjuventude.pt.

 # RECOMMENDED HOTELS

Visitors have a vast range of accommodation options in this part of Portugal. Hotels are scattered across the major towns and resorts of the Algarve, but densely clustered in sprawling resorts that stretch from Lagos to Faro – especially around Portimão, Albufeira and Vilamoura.

Book well in advance for high season, July–September, when hotel beds are difficult to come by. Hotel prices are hugely inflated in the height and heat of summer (though many luxury hotels are also at peak rates around Christmas and New Year). A hotel that is a relatively good bargain in May or October – in many ways the best time to visit the Algarve – may be double or treble the price during the summer months.

Room price guidelines below are *rack rates* for a double room with bath in *high* season, including breakfast and value-added tax. Thus, the prices below may be considerably more than you'll end up paying. All hotels, save for the tiniest residential inns, accept major credit cards. For making reservations, Portugal's country code is 351; the prefixes for the Algarve are 281, 282 and 289.

€€€€€	over €300
€€€€	€200–300
€€€	€120–200
€€	€80–120
€	under €80

SAGRES

Aparthotel Navigator €€ *Rua Infante D. Henrique, Sagres, tel: 282-624 354;* www.aparthotelnavigator.com. This modern hotel, on a cliff right next to the Pousada do Infante, has basic apartments built around a central swimming pool. A good deal for guests who enjoy the low-key, unglitzy appeal of Sagres. Off-season it's an especially good deal. Satellite TV and air-conditioning. Bar, restaurant and squash court. Wheelchair-accessible. 55 apartments.

Hotel Martinhal €€€€ *Quinta do Martinhal, Apartado 54, tel: 282-240 200;* www.martinhal.com. In a breathtaking location overlooking a stretch of rugged coast, this boutique place with great facilities, including tennis courts, has sleekly designed cabins that house spacious beach-facing rooms. There are also villas to rent. 37 rooms.

Hotel Memmo Baleeira €€€ *Vila de Sagres, tel: 282-624 212;* www.memmohotels.com. A large, revamped hotel overlooking the colourful Sagres harbour and within easy striking distance of several sheltered beaches. Contemporary-styled guest rooms with snow-white linen set against silver greys; spa and appealing pool with sea view. 144 rooms.

Pousada do Infante €€–€€€€ *Ponta da Atalaia, 8650 Sagres, tel: 282-620 240;* www.pousadas.pl. Perched on a dramatic clifftop looking out across the Atlantic, this *pousada* (one of three along the Algarve) is prized for its location. Rooms are spacious and comfortable, and most have terraces with excellent views to the coast. Great offers in low season. 51 rooms.

BURGAU

Casa Grande € *Burgau, tel: 282-697 416;* www.casagrandeportugal.com. Unique accommodation in a rambling old villa and converted barn above the slow-moving fishing village of Burgau. Charismatic Sally Vincent, an ex-actress, has been running it since 1972 and will provide you with all you need to know about the region. 7 rooms.

LAGOS

Dom Pedro Meia Praia Beach Club €€€€ *Meia Praia, Lagos, tel: 282-780 400;* www.dompedro.com. This large and popular aparthotel is just across the road from one of the longest stretches of sand along the Algarve coast: Meia Praia, the closest beach to Lagos (3km/2 miles) from town. Well-equipped, airy apartments. Two swimming pools, two tennis courts and landscaped gardens. Good roster of activities and golfing discounts. Wheelchair-accessible. 75 apartments.

Tivoli Lagos €€ *António Crisógono Santos, Lagos, tel: 282-790 079*; www. tivolihotels.com. An excellent choice for those who would prefer to stay in a hotel with character and style in old Lagos rather than on the beach in a generic seaside hotel. Colourful rooms, attractive poolside areas, indoor swimming pool, fitness centre, tennis courts, plus water sports at the Duna Beach Club (hotel transport arranged). Wheelchair-accessible. 324 rooms.

PORTIMÃO AND ENVIRONS

Hotel Oriental €€€ *Avenida Tomás Cabreira, Praia da Rocha, Portimão, tel: 282-480 800*. In the more upscale (and slightly more tranquil) end of Praia da Rocha, this Moorish fantasy palace was designed in the style of the casino that stood on this spot in the 1920s. Features a galleried interior, Turkish bath, pretty gardens with sun terraces, and swimming pools looking onto the beach. Wheelchair-accessible. 90 rooms.

Hotel Bela Vista €€€ *Avenida Tomás Cabreira, Praia da Rocha, Portimão, tel: 282-460 280*; www.hotelbelavista.net. This glorious old mansion overlooks the beach and looks wholly out of place on very built-up Praia da Rocha. An architectural gem, resembling a church more than a hotel, the Bela Vista was built as a summer house in 1916. Its interior features beautiful wood ceilings and staircases, plus splendid 19th-century *azulejos*. It has been thoroughly revamped, additional rooms have been added, and a new spa opened in 2012. 38 rooms.

Penina Golf and Resort €€€ *Montes de Alvor, Portimão, tel: 282-420 200*; www.penina.com. The original luxury golf resort on the Algarve is set within a 145-hectare (360-acre) estate, which includes the world-famous Penina golf course. Perfect for the well-heeled sports lover, with floodlit tennis, watersports, beauty salon and a gym. 188 rooms.

Alvor

Pestana Alvor Praia Hotel €€€ *Praia de Três Irmãos, Alvor, tel: 282-400 900*; www.pestana.com. This large and luxurious hotel sits among thick trees and gardens on cliffs. It overlooks one of the finest beaches along the coast, Praia dos Três Irmãos, which is accessible via elevator and is floodlit at night. Outdoor and indoor seawater pools. Restaurant with terraces and a panoramic view. Tennis courts, full spa, golf and water-sports nearby. Wheelchair-accessible. 198 rooms.

CARVOEIRO

Hotel Carvoeiro Sol €€ *Praia do Carvoeiro, Lagoa, tel: 282-357 301;* http://crimsonhotels.com/hotelcarvoeirosol. Wedged right into the narrow opening between twin cliffs above Carvoeiro's tiny beach, this modern, comfortable hotel has a central courtyard, bar and bright if slightly bland rooms. Wheelchair-accessible. 54 rooms.

MONCHIQUE

Estalagem Abrigo da Montanha € *Estrada Monchique-Fóia, Monchique, tel: 282-912 131;* www.abrigodamontanha.com. High up in the Serra de Monchique, away from the heat and crowds of the coast, this wood-and-granite mountain lodge is a charming place to stay. It's not luxurious, but it has style and spectacular views. Pretty rooftop swimming pool and two restaurants. Slightly more expensive rooms are larger and come with a bigger terrace. 14 rooms.

SILVES

Colina dos Mouros €–€€ *Pocinho Santo, Silves, tel: 282-440 420;* www.colinahotels.com. Located on the outskirts of Silves, this modern hotel has fine views of the fortress and reasonable, spacious rooms with terracotta floors. Landscaped gardens, restaurant, bar and swimming pool. 57 rooms.

ALBUFEIRA/FALÉSIA

Albufeira Jardim € *Cerro da Piedade, Albufeira, tel: 289-570 070;* www.albufeira-jardim.com. A large enclosed complex of whitewashed tour-ist apartments sit on a hill overlooking the sea. They enjoy fine views and a quiet setting, only a 10-minute walk into town. With three pools, shopping, bars and supermarket. All apartments have either a balcony or terrace. Good value. Bus shuttle service to beach and Albufeira town. 175 apartments.

Alfagar Aldeamento Turístico €–€€ *Santa Eulália, Albufeira, tel: 289-540 220;* http://aldeamento.alfagar.com. Eleven hectares (26 acres) of landscaped gardens and a cliff-top walkway surround this good-value holiday apartment complex. One-, two- and three-bedroom apartments are surrounded by facilities, with indoor and outdoor swimming pools, sauna, steam room and much more. Steps down to Santa Eulália beach. 220 apartments.

Clube Humbria €€ *Estrada de Albufeira, Olhos de Água, Albufeira, tel: 289 583 390;* www.clubehumbria.pt. An attractive holiday complex of well-equipped apartments with swimming pools, children's playground, a supermarket and close proximity to the Olhos de Água beach. Minimum stay three nights in summer and all-inclusive. 193 apartments.

Hotel Belver Boa Vista €–€€ *Rua Samora Barros 20, Albufeira, tel: 289-589 175.* Superb setting, built into the cliff at the very western end of town, with a view over the whole of Albufeira. Close enough to walk to town but far enough away to be quiet in high season. Spa, swimming pool and sun terrace. Adults only. 84 rooms.

Hotel Falésia €€€ *Pinhal do Concelho, Praia da Falésia, tel: 289-501 237;* www.falesia.com. A modern hotel that looks like an apartment building on the edge of the Pine Cliffs resort and golf course. Garden-like lobby, pool with waterfall, two tennis courts, some one- and two-bedroom apartments decorated in hues of terracotta. Shuttle to Falésia beach. Over-16s only. Wheelchair-accessible. 169 rooms.

Hotel São Vicente €€ *São Rafael, Albufeira, tel: 289-583 700;* www.hotel saovicentealbufeira.com. A well-kept villa-style small boutique hotel with great ocean views and a short walk from a couple of the prettiest beaches near Albufeira, Castelo and São Rafael. Nice pool, three restaurants. Adults only. 25 rooms.

Hotel Sol e Mar €€ *Rua José Bernadino de Sousa, Albufeira, tel: 289-580 080;* www.grupofbarata.com. A large block hotel in the town centre with somewhat dated rooms but good value given its main asset – it's built right into the cliff on Albufeira's desirable beach. Indoor pool. A popular economy package-tour hotel. 74 rooms.

Residencial Vila Recife € *Rua Miguel Bombarda, 12, Albufeira, tel: 289-583 740;* www.grupofbarata.com. A 2-minute walk from the heart of old Albufeira, a converted private house with a pleasant garden entrance and a pool. The old section of the house has more character than the modern wing. 29 rooms.

Pine Cliffs Hotel & Resort €€€–€€€€€ *Praia da Falésia, tel: 289-500 100;* www.pinecliffshotel.com. One of the Algarve's most distinguished and luxurious developments, recently renovated, surrounded by pines at the top of dramatic cliffs. Handsome Moorish styling, excellent restaurants and extensive sporting facilities, including nine-hole cliff-top golf course, tennis, watersports, semi-private beach, three pools and spa. Luxury 'Golf Suites', plus villas and apartments. Great facilities for children. Wheelchair-accessible. 215 rooms (33 suites, 70 apartments).

Vila Joya €€€€€ *Estrada da Galé, Albufeira, tel: 289-591 795;* www.vila joya.com. Probably the most stylish hotel on the entire coast, this sumptuously decorated small palazzo is full year-round. Ensconced in beautiful gardens, the Moorish-influenced villa is just minutes from the pretty, calm Galé beach. Beautiful bathrooms, public rooms and gourmet restaurant. Most rooms have sea views. Lovely small pool. Reserve several months in advance. 12 rooms.

ALTE

Hotel Alte €–€€ *Estrada de Sta Margarida, Montinho, tel: 289-478 523;* www.altehotel.com. Near the pretty hill village of Alte, this modern 3-star hotel has lovely views of the rural surroundings, good regional cuisine, swimming pool and tennis courts. 30 rooms.

VILAMOURA

Dom Pedro Marina €€€ *Rua Tivoli Lote H4, Vilamoura, Quarteira, tel: 289-381 000;* www.dompedro.com. Impressive hotel with a tropical feel – palm trees, wicker furniture, tile floors and bamboo shades – perched right on the edge of the Vilamoura marina. Nice gardens and swimming pool. Preferential terms for guests at local golf courses. Wheelchair-accessible. 155 rooms.

Tivoli Marina €€€–€€€€ *Vilamoura, tel: 289-303 303;* www.tivolihotels. com. Sandwiched between the marina and the beach, this swish hotel has contemporary rooms decorated in shades of brown, blue, green and orange. Like the resort, though, it also completes its aims very well. Great views, ultra-modern lobby, very good restaurants, state-of-the-art facilities, tennis courts, indoor and outdoor pools and new spa to pamper guests. Wheelchair-accessible. 383 rooms.

VALE DO LOBO

Dona Filipa & San Lorenzo Golf Resort €€€–€€€€ *Vale do Lobo, tel: 289-357 200;* www.donafilipahotel.com. A handsomely appointed hotel that's a favourite of Algarve golfers. Set amid 180 hectares (450 acres), part of the exclusive Vale do Lobo resort, it has elegant traditional rooms and public areas, and guests are permitted exclusive use of the magnificent San Lorenzo golf course nearby, three floodlit tennis courts, heated pool and Kangaroo Village for entertaining small guests. Wheelchair-accessible. 154 rooms.

QUINTA DO LAGO

Hotel Quinta do Lago €€€€€ *Quinta do Lago, Almancil, tel: 289-350 350;* www.quintadolagohotel.com. One of the standard bearers for luxury and leisure in the Algarve, this resort hotel is set amid 800 hectares (2,000 acres) of gardens and woods. Rooms are tastefully and elegantly decorated. Three golf courses wend their fairways through the Ria Formosa Nature Preserve and are among the finest in Europe. Water sports, state-of-the-art spa, pools and beach access across lovely wooden bridge. Distinguished service. Wheelchair-accessible. 141 rooms.

SÃO BRÁS DE ALPORTEL

Casa da Eira €€ *tel: 916 283 680*; http://casaldaeira.nl. This guesthouse is large and attractive, with a pitched red-tiled roof and simple rooms, and surrounded by manicured lawns and gardens. There's a swimming pool.

FARO

Hotel Eva Faro €€€ *Avenida da República, 1, Faro, tel: 289-001 000*; www.tdhotels.com. The Eva is a large, modern block on the edge of the harbour 90 metres (100yds) from pedestrian shopping streets and the old town. Rooms are coolly contemporary and there are two bars and restaurants, health club and rooftop swimming pool. Wheelchair-accessible. 134 rooms.

Hotel Faro €€€ *Praça Dom Francisco Gomes, Faro, tel: 289-830 830*; http://hotelfaro.pt. It's part of Faro's swankiest shopping centre. The hotel is ideally placed – just outside the old town and overlooking a lively plaza and the harbour – and appealingly chic. Wheelchair-accessible. 52 rooms.

OLHÃO

Pensão Bicuar €–€€ *Rua Vasco da Gama 5, tel: 289-714 816*; www.pensionbicuar.com. With wrought-iron balconies, this charming pension has wood-carved beds and 15 antique-decorated rooms. Pleasant roof terrace.

TAVIRA

Casa do Rio € *António Afonso, 39, Tavira, tel: 281-326 578*; www.casa-do-rio.com or www.tavira-inn.com. Small and characterful bed and breakfast in a private home with a pool right on the river in historic Tavira. Minimum stay three nights. No credit cards. Over-18s only. 4 rooms.

O Pequeno Castelo €€ *Poço das Bruxas, Santo Estavão, Tavira, tel: 281-961 692;* www.pequenocastelo.com. On the outskirts of the picturesque town of Tavira, 'the little castle' is a quiet and friendly bed and breakfast with views of the Atlantic from the veranda. Well placed for walks in the countryside. Swimming pool. Minimum stay of three nights. 2 rooms, 2 apartments, and one cottage.

Pousada Convento da Graça €€€–€€€€€ *Rua D. Paio Peres Correia, Tavira, tel: 210 407 680;* www.pousadas.pt. The Algarve's third *pousada*, which opened in 2006, is one of the most desirable places to stay along the entire coast. The hotel is a beautiful conversion of a 16th-century convent, retaining the Renaissance cloister. Guest rooms are elegant and comfortable (some occupy a new wing), the restaurant is noted for locally sourced fish and seafood, and there's a lush swimming pool. 36 rooms.

Quinta do Caracol €€€€ *Rua do São Pedro, tel: 289-322 475;* www.quinta docaracol.com. A gorgeous white-and-blue painted 17th-century farmhouse with lush gardens and a pool, and with rooms furnished in traditional Algarvian style.

Vilacampina €€€ *Sitio de Campina, Luz de Tavira, tel: 281-961 242;* www.vilacampina.pt. Set in lovely countryside, this glamorous bed and breakfast has nine rooms stylishly decked out in pale palettes with shots of colour, and a gorgeous pool surrounded by serene, shaded daybeds. 9 rooms.

ALCOUTIM

Casa Grande Alcaria Cova € *Cx Postal 174-A Pereiro, Alcoutim, tel: 289 842 369;* www.alcariacova.com. This former farmhouse, about 15km (9 miles) from Alcoutim, is the perfect place to relax away from the crowds. The owner offers bicycle or donkey-ride tours and provides regional breakfasts. 4 rooms.

INDEX

INSIGHT ⊙ GUIDES POCKET GUIDE

ALGARVE

First Edition 2017

Editor: Helen Fanthorpe
Author: Neil Schlecht
Head of Production: Rebeka Davies
Picture Editor: Tom Smyth
Cartography Update: Carte
Update Production: AM Services
Photography Credits: Alamy 100; Bigstock
47, 49; Chris Godet/Apa Publications 80;
Dreamstime 6L, 39, 51, 53, 55, 56, 72; Getty
Images 1, 4ML, 5MC, 15, 26, 67, 85, 89, 91, 93;
iStock 4TC, 5M, 6R, 7R, 31, 33, 36, 40, 68, 83,
87, 94; Lydia Evans/Apa Publications 4MC, 5TC,
5MC, 11, 13, 16, 28, 30, 35, 41, 44, 45, 59, 61,
70, 75, 76, 77, 79; Mary Evans Picture Library
21; Public domain 22; Shutterstock 4TL, 5T,
5M, 7L, 18, 43, 60, 63, 65, 73, 97, 98, 102
Cover Picture: Shutterstock

Distribution

UK, Ireland and Europe: Apa Publications
(UK) Ltd; sales@insightguides.com
United States and Canada: Ingram
Publisher Services; ips@ingramcontent.com
Australia and New Zealand: Woodslane;
info@woodslane.com.au
Southeast Asia: Apa Publications (SN) Pte;
singaporeoffice@insightguides.com
Hong Kong, Taiwan and China:
Apa Publications (HK) Ltd;
hongkongoffice@insightguides.com
Worldwide: Apa Publications (UK) Ltd;
sales@insightguides.com

**Special Sales, Content Licensing
and CoPublishing**
Insight Guides can be purchased in bulk
quantities at discounted prices. We can
create special editions, personalised jackets
and corporate imprints tailored to your
needs. sales@insightguides.com;
www.insightguides.biz

Contact us
Every effort has been made to provide
accurate information in this publication,
but changes are inevitable. The publisher
cannot be responsible for any resulting loss,
inconvenience or injury. We would appreciate
it if readers would call our attention to any
errors or outdated information. We also
welcome your suggestions; please contact us
at: hello@insightguides.com
www.insightguides.com